# Praise for *The Open Innovation Marketplace*

"Seldom is there a book on innovation that aims to innovate both the innovation process and the firm itself. This book shoots high *and* delivers! *The Open Innovation Marketplace* is both inspirational and practical. It helps to show how the NIH (not invented here) syndrome can be creatively conquered in a way that honors the role of research. It lays out the foundations for a new kind of twenty-first century firm—the Challenge Driven Enterprise—that is agile, fast, and can leverage capabilities from around the world. This book is a must read not only for R&D managers, but even more so for CEOs and CFOs, especially those CFOs that seek leverage beyond just financial leverage."

—**John Seely Brown**, Cochair, Deloitte Center for the Edge;
  Former Chief Scientist, Xerox Corp; and Director,
  Xerox Palo Alto Research Center (PARC)


"Many people talk about how work is changing, but Alpheus Bingham and Dwayne Spradlin have actually lived it. This fascinating report from the front lines of open innovation is filled with deep insights for all organizations."

—**Thomas Malone**, MIT Sloan School of Management and
  Author of *The Future of Work*


"Alpheus Bingham and Dwayne Spradlin are two of the world's leading authorities on open innovation. I think of no better guides to show us how any business can drive innovation with open challenges. With case studies from pharma to big oil and government to consumer goods, the authors show how any enterprise can harness networks of innovators to create lasting value."

—**David L. Rogers**, Author of *The Network Is Your Customer:
  Five Strategies to Thrive in a Digital Age*

"InnoCentive's pioneering work greatly influenced the way that GlobalGiving structured its marketplace for innovation in the international development sector. This book provides a helpful framework and vocabulary for leaders in any sector to use when developing strategies for open-sourced problem solving. Alpheus Bingham and Dwayne Spradlin have delivered an accessible and lively guide to the current state of Challenge Driven Innovation, and they explore the possibility of using a challenge orientation to transform enterprises, management strategy, and the nature of work itself."

—**Mari Kuraishi**, Cofounder and President, GlobalGiving Foundation

"Although open innovation has the potential to transform your organization's innovation efforts, most books on this burgeoning topic are academic tomes. Fortunately, you hold in your hands a book that cuts through the hype and gives you proven strategies based on real-world experiences with dozens of success stories. If you want to tap into the true power of crowdsourcing and collaboration, read *The Open Innovation Marketplace*. It will open your business...and it will open your mind."

—**Stephen Shapiro**, Author of *24/7 Innovation* and *Personality Poker*

"With global economies slowly recovering and former powerhouse economies showing significant lags, open innovation may hold the overall key to any nation's ultimate productivity. In their book, *The Open Innovation Marketplace*, Alpheus Bingham and Dwayne Spradlin show readers how to harness the power of millions of individuals, acting independently within the global free market system to help business and people everywhere achieve their true growth and potential. The book clearly lays out a pathway to success and shows every leader and participant in today's socially networked world how to create value in today's 'challenge driven' economy for themselves and others. It is a must read."

—**Barry Libert**, Author of *Social Nation* and Chairman and
   Founder, Mzinga

# THE OPEN INNOVATION
# MARKETPLACE

# THE OPEN INNOVATION MARKETPLACE

## Creating Value in the Challenge Driven Enterprise

ALPHEUS BINGHAM
DWAYNE SPRADLIN

Vice President, Publisher: Tim Moore
Associate Publisher and Director of Marketing: Amy Neidlinger
Executive Editor: Jeanne Glasser
Editorial Assistant: Pamela Boland
Development Editor: Russ Hall
Operations Manager: Gina Kanouse
Senior Marketing Manager: Julie Phifer
Publicity Manager: Laura Czaja
Assistant Marketing Manager: Megan Colvin
Cover Designer: Alan Clements
Managing Editor: Kristy Hart
Project Editor: Jovana San Nicolas-Shirley
Copy Editor: Apostrophe Editing Services
Proofreader: Water Crest Publishing
Senior Indexer: Cheryl Lenser
Compositor: Nonie Ratcliff
Manufacturing Buyer: Dan Uhrig

FT Press offers excellent discounts on this book when ordered in quantity for bulk purchases
or special sales. For more information, please contact U.S. Corporate and Government Sales,
1-800-382-3419, corpsales@pearsontechgroup.com. For sales outside the U.S., please contact
International Sales at international@pearson.com.

Printed in the United States of America

First Printing April 2011

ISBN-13: 978-0-13-231183-0
ISBN-10: 0-13-231183-6

Pearson Education LTD.
Pearson Education Australia PTY, Limited.
Pearson Education Singapore, Pte. Ltd.
Pearson Education Asia, Ltd.
Pearson Education Canada, Ltd.
Pearson Educación de Mexico, S.A. de C.V.
Pearson Education—Japan
Pearson Education Malaysia, Pte. Ltd.

*Library of Congress Cataloging-in-Publication Data*

Bingham, Alpheus, 1953-
   The open innovation marketplace : creating value in the challenge-driven enterprise /
Alpheus Bingham, Dwayne Spradlin.
      p. cm.
   1. Technological innovations—Management. 2. Industrial management. 3. Diffusion of
innovations. 4. Research, Industrial—Management. I. Spradlin, Dwayne, 1966- II. Title.
   HD45.B525 2011
   658.4'063—dc22
                            2010053324

*To my many dear friends around the world who see a different and better future and aren't afraid to take the risks to bring it to pass. And finally to my wife, Deidre, who endured more than she usually has to as I was mentally and physically absent, often hunkered out in the barn writing—and then graciously helped me edit the final copy.*
*—Alph*


*To Michelle, my wife, soul mate, and best friend. Without your inspiration, patience, and support, this book would not have been possible. To my children, Mitchell, Matthew, and Mark. More proof that you can do anything when you put your mind to it! And finally to my parents, whose love and confidence in me never waned. Thank you.*
*—Dwayne*

# Contents

**PART II**    **The Challenge Driven Enterprise: Virtualizing the Business Model to Drive Innovation, Agility, and Value Creation**

# Foreword

by Christopher Meyer

Most likely, you picked up this book because you're interested in innovation. You won't be disappointed—you'll find here a tightly reasoned rationale for the spread of open innovation, use cases in large corporations, not-for-profit, and government and practical guidance for employing this approach yourself. Your guides are two experienced entrepreneurs—one an accomplished big-company executive, one a serial startup veteran—who founded an open innovation business whose success required them to conquer one of the business world's great challenges—get big companies to change their behavior.

But ten years from now *Open Innovation Marketplace* will be remembered for two broader contributions. The book describes the appearance of a new species in the evolution of an information-based economy: a global network of highly specialized expertise, on tap whenever, wherever, it's needed. The authors then interpret the resulting operating changes in innovation processes in light of the new economics of information and labor. But that's only the first act: In the second, the authors look through the other end of the telescope to see what these changes imply for corporate organizations *beyond* the innovation process. They don't stop until they've described a new model of organization fit for the information economy.

Where does InnoCentive (the authors' company) fit in this story of a new economy? In the 1990s, it was often repeated that "the Internet changes everything." Clearly, though, it doesn't change everything at once. New economies don't spring full-blown from the head of Zeus—they follow a somewhat predictable life cycle, in which new science leads to new technology, which business eventually embraces. Nineteenth century work in the sciences of thermodynamics and chemistry, for example, led to technologies for steelmaking and petroleum refining, and then to new products, such as automobiles and air conditioners. And because the companies optimized for mass-production required thousands, not dozens, of people, new organizational forms arose to manage activity on this scale, creating the corporate organizational form we took for granted 20 years ago. To get full value from this book, keep this in mind: The corporate organization form that dominated the twentieth century was the solution to a particular challenge—create a structure that can attract capital at a large scale (hence limited liability), achieve the economies of scale the new technology enables (with assembly lines, three shifts, and so on), and coordinate the activities of large numbers of people (using functional hierarchies, cost accounting systems, and company towns).

These arrangements solved a problem that was pressing around 1900. Today we have a new one.

As Stan Davis and I wrote in *BLUR*,[1] following the same cycle as industrialization, we're now approaching the fourth stage of the development of the Information Economy. The fundamental sciences of semiconductors and information theory, explored prior to 1950, begat an information technology industry—microprocessors, fibers, routers, software, and the rest. Consequently, today's businesses are learning to leverage information the way their industrial forebears leveraged energy. The result is a new infrastructure for the economy—just as railroads, national highways, and ubiquitous service stations composed a new "transportation sector," we now have semiconductor fabs, ISPs, Geek Squads, and the rest of our information industries. The economy is "informationalizing," the way it previously industrialized. And an important milestone: As autos and appliances distributed industrial technology to individuals, PCs, game consoles, and smartphones have equipped everyone—increasingly, globally, *everyone*—to participate in the information economy.

What we don't have quite yet is an organizational form that solves the new challenges to create value in an informationalized world.

If the Information Economy is approaching its fourth "quarter," we should now be seeing new approaches to organizing economic activity that depart from earlier structures and provide a leap in productivity as the large, functionally organized industrial corporation did. What are the challenges to which these structures must respond in this cycle? They include the reduced cost of communicating anytime, anyplace; the competitive need to accelerate innovation; and the existence of a talent pool distributed widely around the world. Perhaps most important: The unique economics of digitally encoded information that can now be reproduced at essentially zero marginal cost. And seeing them we are.

Linux, the icon of open source software development, became available in 1992.[2] This, too, was a major milestone. First, it demonstrated the practicality of self-organization, creating valuable output through the group adoption of a set of rules rather than through the orchestrated operation of a formal organization. Second, it pioneered a definition of property foreign to the industrial economy: valuable stuff, shared for free.

Not surprisingly, this excited considerable resistance from people making money from digital property, and a decade later the IP wars are far from over in the software, music, movie, or pharmaceutical industries. Nonetheless, leading-edge companies saw the upside in the capability to economically involve skilled, motivated contributors around the world that the Linux community demonstrated. But it took some time to figure out some combinations of governance structures and commercial arrangements that could take advantage of the economics of networks without sacrificing the capability to earn a profit. Around 2000, Procter & Gamble started its "Connect and Develop" approach to innovation. And InnoCentive was founded in 2001.

It's not coincidental that these developments both centered on innovation. One of the consequences of the connected economy is the acceleration of change itself.[3] In the mature industrial world, the rule "if it ain't broke, don't fix it" made good sense, for business models and for machines. Change was something that happened seldom, was expected to disrupt an organization, and usually was driven by a single novel pressure—Japanese competition in the 1980s, say, or the Quality Movement. Now, innovation capability is coming to be seen as the most productive asset—for an individual, a company, or a country. In 1980, the question "What's your business model?" would have made you sound like an idiot—now it makes you sound smart.

Because networks accelerate innovation, they also increase the need for it. And the information economy has responded: Innovation used to be a captive function, the purview of R&D groups and strategy officers. Now a new sector of the global economy has emerged, devoted to innovation: VCs, angels and angel funds; legal and accounting practices devoted to startups; corporate venture funds; specialized journals and conferences; and business plan competitions, patent exchanges, and even a new and prestigious profession: serial entrepreneur. (Prestigious, that is, in innovative economies. In Spain, failing at a venture brings shame on your family.)

InnoCentive is a part of this new sector. Its story is important because it is one of the early examples of applying the economics of connectivity, search, and self-organization to an established business function, finding a radically different solution and making it pay.

The authors here share their unique story, but they have a broader point. Networked innovation is indeed one of the new, needed solutions, but it's more than that: It's a pathfinder. InnoCentive's success forces us to ask, how do its principles apply to every function of an organization? And when, collectively, we answer this question, what will be left of the organization form we're used to? What can we learn from this case about the next organizational solution? In the second half of this book, Bingham and Spradlin take on this question as well.

In the late 1990s, Alph Bingham and I used to speculate about the economy as intersecting networks of capabilities: an "economic web" of companies, and an "organization web" of capabilities inside them. We discussed the increasing permeability of the boundary between the two webs, and the expectation that communications technology would eventually make it so porous that they would merge. The advanced economies remain far from that vision, but InnoCentive is poking new holes in this boundary every day—it is both the product of information technology and the agent of change in informationalized organization. Alph and Dwayne have an unmatched perspective on the fine-grained work it takes to make this kind of progress, a clear-eyed view of what will be possible next, and a deep understanding of the forces impelling the changes.

As William Gibson says, "The future is already here, it's just unevenly distributed." If it hasn't reached you before, it's arrived in this volume.

# Acknowledgments

The authors want to extend a sincere thank-you to those who contributed to this manuscript and without which it would never have been possible. First, thanks to Leah Spiro, a tireless project coach and editor that held our feet to the fire and still took all our copy at the latest possible moment. Confusing thoughts are all ours. She tried, and did the best with what she had to work with (sic). Case studies were assembled by Andrea Meyer and John Dila, which helped make our intervening text come to life. Anne Greenberg checked the facts. And duly warned us when she could not. And not least, we want to thank our publisher, Pearson Education and its team of editors and especially Jeanne Glasser who saw something in an early outline, now barely recognizable.

A special thanks to Eli Lilly and Company, and some key, risk-taking executives for launching and supporting what have become some of the most unusual "laboratories" in which novel innovation models are being tested and proven, InnoCentive, among them.

We could not begin to thank those friends, colleagues, InnoCentive board members and advisors, whose genius provoked us, challenged us and inspired us. It happened over decades and goes on to this very moment.

# About the Authors

**Alpheus Bingham** is a pioneer in the field of open innovation and an advocate of collaborative approaches to research and development. He is co-founder and former president and chief executive officer of InnoCentive.

Alpheus spent more than 25 years with Eli Lilly and Company; he retired as vice president of e.Lilly and vice president of Research Strategy. He had formerly been the vice president of Sourcing Innovation. He served on both the R&D Policy Committee and the corporate Operations Committee. He has deep experience in pharmaceutical research and development, research acquisitions and collaborations, and R&D strategic planning. During his career, he was instrumental in creating and developing Lilly's portfolio management process and establishing the divisions of Research Acquisitions, the Office of Alliance Management, and e.Lilly, a business innovation unit, from which was launched various other ventures that create the advantages of open and networked organizational structures, including InnoCentive, YourEncore, Inc., Coalesix, Inc., Maaguzi, Inc., Indigo Biosystems, Seriosity, Chorus, and Collaborative Drug Discovery, Inc.

He currently serves on the Board of Directors of InnoCentive and Collaborative Drug Discovery, Inc.; the advisory boards of the Center for Collective Intelligence at MIT and the Business Innovation Factory, and as a member of the board of trustees of the Bankinter Foundation for Innovation in Madrid.

He has lectured extensively at both national and international events and serves as a Visiting Scholar at the National Center for Supercomputing Application at the University of Illinois at Champaign-Urbana. He is also the former chairman of the Board of Editors of the *Research Technology Management Journal*. Alpheus was the recipient of The Economist's Fourth Annual Innovation Summit "Business Process Award" for InnoCentive. He was also named as one of Project Management Institute's "Power 50" leaders in October 2005.

Alpheus received a B.S. degree in chemistry from Brigham Young University and a Ph.D. degree in organic chemistry from Stanford University.


**Dwayne Spradlin** has been on the forefront of business innovation and leadership for more than 20 years. He is intensely focused on two areas: finding new ways to unleash and focus human potential using technology and defining the role of leadership in driving change in our businesses and culture.

Dwayne serves as president and chief executive officer at Inno-Centive, the global leader in Open Innovation. Previous positions have included president of Hoovers Online, president and COO of StarCite, senior vice president of Corporate Development Vertical-Net, and director at PriceWaterhouseCoopers, where he spent ten years delivering Technology and Strategy solutions to Fortune 500 clients including Intel, Compaq, Caremark, and United Airlines. Dwayne currently sits on the Board of Directors of both InnoCentive and Cortera.

Considered an authority on crowdsourcing, Open Innovation, and the role of Innovation in Philanthropy, Dwayne has been a keynote speaker at events on five continents, He is frequently interviewed and has been featured on CNBC, ABC, NPR, and BBC and quoted in the *Economist, BusinessWeek, The New York Times*, and many other journals and periodicals.

Dwayne holds a B.A. degree in applied mathematics and an M.B.A. degree from the University of Chicago. He lives in Southlake, TX, with his wife and three children.

# Preface

Open innovation is actually a pretty straightforward concept. It's the use of resources other than those internal to an organization, contributing in a meaningful way to an innovative outcome associated—owned if you will—by the organization that benefits directly from its distribution in the marketplace. But, as we unpack the business implications, as we examine the decision processes, as we look more closely at the organizational consequences, it is clearly a profound subject about which much has been and will be written. We feel that our contribution to that body of literature and practice is uniquely informed. As executives of InnoCentive, we have used our own business as a laboratory for understanding open processes and for examining the way innovation is practiced by ourselves and our many customers and partners, as well as the historic practices of the organizations in which we had been previously engaged. And, we strive to continually update our understanding of how and why it actually works to improve on that process for the success of our business and for the success of our customers.

InnoCentive was launched in 2001. At that time, there was no crowdsourcing or broadcast search channel to turn to for business innovation. In fact, those terms hadn't even been coined yet. Eli Lilly and Company saw the potential for making a change in the way they innovated. They recognized that distributed in an unsearchable crowd were insights, flashes of genius, and ideas that would never be evident on job applications, resumes, or consulting brochures. They would hinge upon the uniqueness of every human experience and the chaotic way in which "aha moments" are distributed among persons of widely varying academic and career qualifications. Lilly saw the potential for tapping that ingenuity and a new business model was born. It became another "channel" in what was emerging as a rapidly growing world of innovation alternatives to "doing it yourself."

As we worked to create a successful business around this new model, new language sprang up to characterize it. We already mentioned the subsequent coining of the terms "crowdsourcing" by Jeff Howe and "broadcast search" by Karim Lakhani. Internally InnoCentive used familiar terms in very deliberate ways. Our customers, providing challenging problems to our network, became "Seekers." And our network was one of "Solvers." The problems themselves were "Challenges." And we used these descriptions as we analyzed questions like: What was the value proposition to Seekers? Why did Solvers engage? And how did the properties of the Challenge serve to effectively contribute to its solution? As we authored this book, we were aware that sometimes we meant seeker as one who seeks a solution and sometimes we meant it as a specific player in a business ecology, an entity with the titular role of Seeker. We have striven to be consistent in our use of capitals. In the end, we realized there was no perfect solution. Any single, albeit consistent, default to a rule felt awkward at times. We used our judgment. We hope it worked.

These new approaches to innovation—crowdsourcing, broadcast search, electronic requests for proposals, and public-private partnerships—were joining the more historic ranks of joint ventures, contract labs, university research, and consulting services as a growing number of channels for innovation. The new modalities were being added faster than the techniques for orchestrating and managing them were. Taken altogether, these many marketplaces, platforms, and exchanges were becoming an innovation marketplace—an Open Innovation Marketplace. And in this sense, open means not just external, it means open to any source of contribution, including the efforts of the internal staff and innovation contributors. In the chapters that follow, we will present rationale for why open is better. We will present a framework for creating value in this market reality and rethinking your innovation processes. We will show how to select appropriate channels when faced with the myriad choices and we will discuss the ways this may transform the very organizational structure of our business as these principles flow throughout.

Like most books, you can pick this one up, turn to page 1, and read it straight through. But inasmuch as we have chosen as our audience executives, foundation leaders, project managers, agency heads, and business students, we have architected the book in such a way that it also serves as its own synopsis.

After the introduction, each chapter is followed by a case study. You can read the chapter's opening quote, the first paragraph or two, under the subheading "Overview" and the subsequent case study. In this way, the concepts are brought to life through the stories—and theoretical details and background can be later filled in as chosen. Those who might elect to read as such, should also read the synopsis of Chapters 1–8 that appears in the beginning of Chapter 9, "Leadership."

Two chapters stand somewhat separate from the remainder. These two are intended to serve as a practicum to the main body of the text. Chapter 5, "The Selection of Appropriate Innovation Channels," establishes a decision-making tool for selecting innovation channels after a project's properties are defined. And Chapter 8, "The Challenge Driven Enterprise Playbook," serves as a playbook for change and the transformation to a more virtual organization we refer to as the "challenge driven enterprise." We recommend that they at least be skimmed for their structure even if the details are to be executed by others in the organization. And, be sure to read the critical case studies at the end of Chapter 5 and Chapter 8.

Though sources are cited, as appropriate, in the notes at the end of each chapter, we have also compiled a reading list of texts and papers that can augment the content and provide better grounding in topics that could only be covered in brief.

# 1

## Introduction

"The race is not always to the swift, nor the battle to the strong, but that's the way to bet."

—*Damon Runyon*

## Placing Bets

The proclivity to bet on the "swift" might serve you well, especially when it comes to placing bets at the racetrack. But in a new and complex world, few people actually know what "swift" or "strong" means in every context. For example, an executive may know what a "strong" market analyst or a "strong" manufacturing department head looks like when it comes to hiring someone. Yet that same executive might find it hard to identify a "strong" pharmacokineticist, which is a new, highly specialized branch of pharmacology. Indeed, it's because of this difficulty that universities issue PhDs in pharmacokinetics. You can assume that if people have a PhD, they are certified as "strong," even if you can't make that assessment on your own.

But in today's heavily connected world, what if, instead of relying on handicappers like universities to help you improve your odds, you could sometimes place your bets *after* the race is run? Wouldn't this render measurements of "swift and strong" utterly moot? After all, you would know who WON. Not who might have won or even *should* have won but who actually won. This contrarian notion is one of several at the heart of this book and will be further developed as the numerous present-day channels, or modalities, of innovation are elaborated and how you can more effectively make these choices and manage them.

Who is this book for? It is directed to the decision makers who are ultimately accountable for driving business performance and innovation in their organizations. These leaders have many different titles and specific roles. They are CEOs, company founders, chief scientific officers, foundation directors, government agency heads, and policy makers, to name a few. They run an equally broad range of entities, from a not-for-profit foundation seeking cures for orphan diseases, to a corporate business unit bringing a new product to market, to a government agency seeking breakthroughs to better provide security for its citizens.

Innovation processes and approaches are undergoing significant change—in business, in philanthropy, and in government. A new lexicon is emerging to describe these changes: terms such as, open innovation, crowdsourcing, prize philanthropy, public-private partnerships, broadcast search, and so on. Through years of practitioner experience with real-world clients, the authors have developed an approach that we call **Challenge Driven Innovation** (CDI) which is the focus of Part I. CDI brings an approach and rigor. It reframes the innovation and business process in light of the many new channels and partnerships available. And, it helps guide innovation leaders at all levels in the selection of those channels. This is an approach with enough precision to drive innovation, but agile enough to create value everywhere in the organization. We believe that organizations that adopt CDI pervasively essentially virtualize the enterprise and will have an even greater opportunity to drive business performance and market leadership in the twenty-first century. We call that vision the **Challenge Driven Enterprise** (CDE), the focus of Part II.

What can a business expect from the full adoption and strategic practice of Challenge Driven Innovation? Nothing less than the following:

- More cost effective problem solving
- A greater diversity of approaches to innovation
- Better management of risk
- Not reinventing the wheel
- Accelerated innovation
- Ability to pay for results and not just efforts

## Managing the Innovation Process

How business, philanthropy, and government leaders direct the research and development (R&D) resources of their organizations to foster innovation is a critical part of their overall leadership. And, it is crucial to the market performance of many institutions. Ultimately, this leadership and its consequential innovations play a bigger role in society: These innovations underpin the quality of life of every person on earth. Think about it: It was innovation, defined as creativity and implementation, that created efficient farm practices to better feed people, water purification to minimize disease, educational advances to better the understanding of the world, the printing press, the steam engine, the Internet—a near endless list of human advances.

Within the walls of various corporate, nonprofit, and governmental departments charged with innovation are "the geese that have laid the golden eggs." These "eggs" are the products and ideas on which the company was built and on which it subsequently thrived. And the "geese?" Well, they're the scientists, designers, technologists, artists—the "creatives" that produced those eggs in the past and are counted on to produce them in the future. Organizational culture and lore often suggest that, "many leaders don't understand the mysterious innovation process and are as likely to kill those geese as to nourish them," or so the thinking goes. Given this reality, it certainly seems risky for a non-R&D leader to tinker with that part of the organization—"let's just leave it to others," is a too often accepted groupthink.

But if leaders had this attitude toward operating divisions such as marketing or manufacturing, it would rarely be tolerated. And yet, for the sanctum sanctorum, areas like R&D and product development, somehow it seems OK. It's not. Some would simply call this hands-off behavior a dereliction of duty. Whatever you call it, truth be known, the scientists and technical leaders in these innovation departments *like* this status quo and resist change.

We also want to assure you that we are ever mindful that innovation is hardly a strictly R&D phenomenon. Innovation spans across all areas of a business. Innovative solutions are, of course, needed for new product lines and product improvements. But, we can also talk about innovative marketing campaigns, innovative business strategies, innovative manufacturing processes, and innovative sales approaches. None of that is even a stretch. We must therefore ask that this broad notion of innovation be kept in mind. We sometimes use terms specific to technology or engineering, but that is to allow the use of specific examples, concrete language, and clarity. We sometimes, but not always, use broader language or multiple role descriptors as a reminder of our intention and awareness. Most importantly, the principles we discuss will have application in the broader sense, and that breadth is a key to understanding the CDE, central to Part II of this book.

This book uses a fairly well-established definition of innovation: an event characterized by an act of creation or invention followed by successful implementation and deployment so that the benefits of that creation may be widely enjoyed. By defining innovation as "realized invention," you can create two distinct subevents which, in practice, have their own separate set of properties, conditions, and approaches. Of the two events, creation/invention and implementation/realization, the second act of implementation, or realization, is the one most amenable to processes, structure, and what you would classically think of as managerial intervention.

The first, the creation or invention part, has always been and remains a bit murkier. When you imagine your own personal experience with innovation, it is always much easier to describe to others the implementation part. Just how you went about inventing something isn't perfectly clear even to you. How can you manage the invention process when it just seems to happen? Surely the "conditions" were right. And so, much effort is given to the managerial duties of creating the right environment. How else to explain all those beanbag chairs on corporate invoices in the 1990s that were supposed to kick-start out-of-the-box ideas?

So, on the one hand, invention seems to be a tricky thing to manage and best left to the inventors. At the same time, we openly accuse general managers of dereliction of duty for having anything less than a robust management strategy for their innovation functions. How can managers resolve this contradiction?

## Balancing a Portfolio

The answer isn't all that complicated as an oversimplistic metaphor can demonstrate. A billboard recently seen in Nevada, where gambling is legal, advertised prime rib dinners with the price of $7.77, showing as three winning numbers on a slot machine. Yet think about slot machines and the casino business. You never know each time you pull the handle or press the button of a slot machine whether you are a winner or a loser. Yet, in spite of the unpredictability of any given play or even any given machine, few casino owners worry about losing money across the casino. The methods for managing systems of probabilities and unpredictable processes have been around for a long time; however, they need to be applied with greater rigor to the innovation processes, on which we survive.

Now, of course, you can fully appreciate that the notion of managing innovation as a portfolio of opportunities is hardly novel. But we can and should explore more deeply the relationship between innovation portfolio management and the historical growth of "open innovation," which is the use of invention sources independent of the organization charged with delivering the innovation to the marketplace. This phenomenon was defined, and its substantial business impact analyzed in the seminal work *Open Innovation*[1] by Professor Henry Chesbrough and to which we refer the reader for a deeper grounding. What are the strategic opportunities created by a more deliberate integration of the role of "open innovation" into the overall portfolio? When you use the term **portfolio**, you must, of necessity, mean a *balanced* portfolio. And actually, since a portfolio would be nothing more than a *collection* in the absence of that adjective, "balanced" is always implied. And so what is it that "unbalances" your portfolio? In later chapters, we spend far more time on the topic of diversity, so all those arguments aren't replicated here. But internally generated projects are bound to possess a certain sameness. Thus, balancing is likely to demand an openness to external ideas, external projects, and external products—namely, ones that originate outside the organization.

Sourcing of more projects from outside the organization is *not* just a numbers game. Do not trivialize these arguments as merely the admonition to "take more shots on goal." Plenty of analyses from the sports world suggests that the higher *scoring* team makes a higher *percentage* of attempted shots as well. The processes used to manage a portfolio of innovative ideas must be well designed and rigorously applied, but the tools and specifics—that is, pareto diagrams, decision-trees, and option theories—deliberately remain beyond the scope of this book. The focus of this book is not "how" to manage a portfolio. It is rather to show that new innovation channels offer a portfolio balancing capability, and therefore a desirable outcome, unavailable with internal projects alone. This notion that a diverse portfolio of assets predictably outperforms a more correlated one is an important concept and one which is approached from multiple angles.

Beyond the factor of diversity, a second factor linking open innovation and innovation portfolio management is risk. There are many complex and valuable ways you can address the topic of risk and far more is said and written about risk than is done to contain it. When advancing an innovation portfolio, you need to worry about three kinds of risk: financial, technical, and execution. Closed innovation systems, where all the invention and creation takes place within the walls of a single institution, compel the innovator to load all this risk into one organizational basket. And that cumulative risk too often results in a "bet the farm" scenario. This risky strategy has resulted in the disappearance of many fine companies across numerous sectors. The pharmaceutical sector stands as a notable example. Think of the various medicines you and your family have taken. Many of the original producers, of well-known products like Motrin, no longer exist as individual entities, including SmithKline, Beecham, Ciba-Geigy, Roussel, Hoechst, Marion, and Merrel. What happened to Parke-Davis, Upjohn, Burroughs, and a host of others? These brands no longer exist. The executive teams no longer exist. The stock in those companies no longer exists. And although the answer is complex and has many elements idiosyncratic to those specific institutions, it is also a generally true statement that their demise could be traced to an over-accumulation of risk within their business entity.

The simple point to be drawn is that open innovation provides an invaluable means to balance an innovation portfolio and share risks. The consequences are so significant that all business leaders should be actively charged to attend to the innovation process and its strategic role.

Now recognize that the implementation of an actively managed innovation strategy won't be without obstacles. Scientists generally prefer to be ignored by process-mongers, portfolio managers, and others who might not be there with an agenda that is fully aligned with theirs, which is, first and foremost, peeling away nature's layers of obscurity. Similar comments could be made about the resistance of technologists or artists. Although there might be plenty of opportunity to talk about the underlying reasons that these creative types, as a whole, have a tenuous relationship with authority, we would rather focus on how the overall systems tend to be biased toward flawed portfolio management. We will look next at how corporate culture and organizational myths distort attempts to effectively manage a portfolio of innovative projects with uncertain outcomes and a frequently low probability of success.

## False Positives Versus False Negatives

An actively managed portfolio demands judgment calls. The judgments may well be based on quantitative values and careful measurements. But unless you have nearly inexhaustible resources and can see every risky project through to its final conclusion, imperfect judgments will have to be made, running the risk of being wrong. Two simple criteria for effective portfolio management are to make judgments as early as possible and to make as few errors as possible. When speaking of errors in this context, you need to classify two types of error, often referred to as alpha errors and beta errors or, in other contexts, false positives and false negatives, and sometimes just as simply as type I and type II errors.

In a portfolio, a false positive is a project deemed to be "successful" and that gets resources, and advances, but that ultimately fails. A false negative is a project terminated on the assumption that it will fail and then ultimately proves successful. Although each type of error is easy enough to make, it is harder to track false negatives because after a project is terminated, it is only occasionally reincarnated to prove its ultimate worth. A typical false-negative scenario is one in which the project is terminated, with regard to the expenditure of resources, but is licensed elsewhere, and the licensee ultimately succeeds. When good judgments are made under conditions of incomplete and imperfect knowledge, both these types of error *must* occur. Logically, any attempt to eliminate one error type results in a greater number of instances of the other type. So if you never want to make the error of a false positive, you need to ruthlessly terminate projects with any hint of potentially failing—to avoid unnecessarily committing resources to them. Thus, you create many more false negatives in the process.

Well-managed portfolios result in both types of error. But what are the cultural pressures that might result in an overcommitment of one error type and consequently the commission of too many errors overall? Naturally, no innovator, whether scientist, technologist, or artist, wants to see their project terminated. So, not surprisingly, there is pressure to commit the error of falsely identifying a project as positive when it ultimately will fail. Consistent with this pressure—and serving the interest of individual project leaders and team members—most organizations have generated highly adverse stories about "the one that got away."

This doesn't mean that false negatives are somehow good. All errors are costly: The false positive error consumes resources and capital that, if deployed elsewhere, could have benefited the organization and its customers; and false negatives represent the very project in which the application of additional resources and capital would have served the organization and its customers. Remember that a bias toward one type of error will increase the total error population, and because both types of error represent cost without return, the goal clearly has to be to keep the sum of all errors as low as possible. Errors *are* a natural part of decision making under uncertainty, but they can be managed well or poorly, and good decision processes are often the difference between your ultimate success versus a competitor's.

# Rationalizing Innovation Failure

How this error type preference works in real organizational life is that the story about the "one that got away" is relayed with such anxiety that every project with an uncertain outcome is identified as yet another example of one which you may "let get away." This vigilance to avoid any future embarrassment of the false negative results in a host of projects kept alive well beyond their time.

To rationalize this portfolio-inefficient mentality, a variety of other behaviors surface throughout the organization. Researchers wanting to avoid their pet projects being terminated identify closely with this tale, and research leaders adopt the mantra, "we can't afford to at least not try." Leaders outside the research departments are drafted to get on board by having it patiently explained to them that waste is a completely natural part of the research process and can't be avoided if one is to do great things. All parties can count on pithy snippets of history to aid and abet them in this effort. Even the venerable "wizard of Menlo Park," Thomas Edison, dismissed his critics by insisting that his failures were an integral part of his success by proudly declaring that shareholder investment had absolutely *not* been wasted because he now knew "10,000 ways not to make a light bulb."

None of this is to say that there is some magic formula by which research will just progress from one success to another, or that at some high standard of portfolio management, payment for failure magically disappears. We challenge these institutionalized versions of R&D simply because they have become so entrenched that they are all but invisible and leaders are too quick to accept the "nature of the beast" as part of institutional lore. Making these myths apparent is only a tiny first step to more effectively addressing them. And what should now be clear is that the addressing of these issues is the responsibility of all organizational leadership and not just those directly charged with executing the innovation projects upon which the future of the organization inevitably rests.

# Portfolio Management and Open Innovation

After promising to tie this issue of portfolio management to open innovation, it may appear that this promise was sidetracked. Not so. One important component of open innovation is that it creates an opportunity to share risks and expenses with external parties. The adverse consequences of the false positive are effectively neutralized when someone else is underwriting some or all of the costs. Details of how you can manage this risk-sharing, and the organizational structures that support it, will be covered in subsequent chapters. But, for now, error minimization, portfolio management, and open innovation need to be integrated into a total innovation management system that copes effectively with risk and probability, and that manages to a desirable economic outcome.

Many companies—and even whole industry sectors—compete primarily on the basis of innovation, for example, pharmaceutical companies that must routinely invent new medicines or the advertising industry that constantly must come up with snappy original taglines. Innovation is what enables these companies to maintain a competitive "edge" as opposed to competing on price, convenience, added services, or some other aspect of business. Even as the argument is made for other modes of competing, one cannot help but be reminded that convenience, services, and low-pricing is often the opportunity presented by an innovation of some type. No, the reality in the twenty-first century is that virtually all businesses are months away from a wave of novel competitors. Innovative companies survive.

Historically, innovation competition has revolved around each company's capability to assemble creative departments—and most important, teams of exceptional talent that strive to out-innovate their competition. This was accomplished by smart people, with excellent equipment and facilities, inventing new products—and even new technologies—and often making fundamental advances in science.

Think Bell Labs as a prototype. Of course, even though Bell Labs continues as a distinct entity, it has not fully survived in the form that characterized it in its heyday because it has been altered by spinoffs, layoffs, mergers, and mission changes.

No doubt many factors contributed to the transformation of the central lab, with a broad remit for science. It is not the intent to thoroughly analyze Bell Labs or even to propose a scholarly hypothesis to explain its mutation. Surely some of those factors must include the broader access to knowledge because of the "information age." Business, also, has become more sophisticated in its capability to locate and license ideas. This decreased the need to invent it all in-house. The adage that "none of us is as smart as all of us" has been scaled up and globalized.

Even so, an enormous percentage of the applied science and technology, and ultimately, "reduction to practice" remained an internal skill. Responding to this reality, a significant number of graduating scientists, engineers, and technologists historically went to work for large corporations—as did designers, graphic artists and draftsmen. The shift to "distributed innovation" has taken place slowly—over decades—until today, when many sectors can point to significant fractions of their new product introductions and underlying technologies as originating outside of their corporate labs. **Distributed innovation** is a gathering of ideas and solutions from many quarters and the integration of the pieces, by a central organization into what would be considered the final innovation. Some, such as Procter & Gamble, have even declared this as a strategic intent, one they call "Connect and Develop," or C+D. They have set quantitative goals to increase licensing as the primary mode of innovation growth while maintaining a more constant level of internal R&D resources. This initiative is one you learn more about in the case study at the conclusion of Chapter 6, "The Challenge Driven Enterprise."

Now is the era of "Open Innovation." The shift to contract labs and licensed technologies is currently the major part of the open innovation movement. But recent increases in broadband Internet access and other leaps in communication enable you to imagine a future in which technical problem solving, on the spot invention, and on-demand innovation can be realized—maybe even predominantly—through open communities of scientists. Examples of these open innovation communities are InnoCentive, the authors' company, and TopCoder. These enabling platforms, and their attendant business entities, in which the network is managed on behalf of other institutions, have been named **innomediators** by Professor Mohanbir Sawhney at Northwestern University's Kellogg School of Management.

Later chapters discuss how the various innovation channels are selected, how they play off against one another, and how they are ultimately integrated for innovation. Putting all this together ushers in new organizational and partnering realities: Marketplaces in which intellectual property—with or without its legal appendages—is exchanged as readily as Hummels on eBay. Maybe that's a bit of an exaggeration in 2011, but stay tuned.

## Exploration Versus Exploitation

The need to constantly challenge your assumptions and your frame of reference was previously mentioned. Especially because time and familiarity renders your assumptions and frames of reference invisible, even to yourself.

I am reminded of how stubborn some of my own biases were at a conference sponsored by the Santa Fe Institute. The speaker was David Stark, a sociologist at Colombia University. He began with a story of the Naskapi Indians, a tribe native to Labrador. Inasmuch as this was a conference for business executives, and not sociologists or anthropologists, it was clear that his story was to be a metaphor for teaching a concept to the business community. I sat listening to the story and imagining the message that was to follow. I thought I had it completely figured out. And the wrongness of my conclusions reminded me of the extent to which certain patterns of analyses had crept in and prevented me from seeing things in a fresh light.

Stark's story told of the elk feasts during the hunting season when all the village would gather to prepare and to share the elk meat brought in by the young hunters. At the conclusion of each feast, the shoulder bone from the day's catch was waved over the camp-fire until it was mottled with soot. The partially blackened shoulder blade was handed to the tribe's shaman who interpreted the marks as a map that would guide the hunters to elk the next day. Listening to this story, I concluded that it must be an allegory for the wisdom of the corporate elders. Yes, I admit, I was getting old and quickly imagined this was a reminder that the brash, youthful ideas just imported along with newly minted MBA degrees required the tempering of experience and wisdom to be effectively implemented.

Wow! Did I get it wrong.

The *actual* conclusion and lesson to be taken from the Naskapi ritual was that the shaman didn't have the faintest idea what the patterns meant nor where the elk would be foraging on the following day. The entire ritual served only to inject an element of randomness into the hunt—randomness that sometimes led to the discovery of new populations of elk; but more often, led to the hunters returning empty-handed at the end of the next day. And yet, over time this failure was interpreted to have led to the longer-term sustainability of both tribe and elk by avoiding what would have been the inevitable hunting out of entire elk populations—by hunters who measured their immediate worth only in terms of bringing in fresh kill. Stark then told other stories further establishing the relationship between survivability and the exploration-exploitation balance.

Although many of you may have immediately divined the correct message in the shaman's reading of the shoulder bone, my own inability to see it was insured by more than one bias as the story unfolded. First, there is a tendency to perceive randomness as a "bad" thing—a symptom that something is out of control. We strive to make our world ever more deterministic and ever more predictable, and randomness seems evidence of failure—the same sense of failure felt by the young hunters more concerned with their reputation on the morrow than they were about the preservation of the food supply for decades into the future. The intention here is not to go down the sidetrack of corporate shortsightedness, as tempting as it is to take pot shots at that target-rich environment. Rather, the point is this: Today's technologies make *exploring* for innovative ideas easier than ever before, while at the same time, today's competitive and economic realities make the bias toward pure *exploitation* harder to resist than ever before. As our organizations strive to articulate clear strategies for innovation, it is crucial that they maintain a balance between exploration and exploitation.

Just as the random soot patterns created the ability for the Naskapi to explore unknown regions, so too, do the various modes of open innovation enable organizations to explore unknown and unbiased, or at least differently biased, regions of technology, design, or policy, in ways previously too costly or too difficult.

## Meta-Innovation

In examining the broad topic of open innovation a little more deeply, you find that some innovation modalities or innovation channels have been around a long time. One example would be the specialty labs that have long been used for customized testing or analyses or to which selected operations may be outsourced. On the other hand, some open innovation modalities are newer, with only limited examples of historical use: for instance, tech-scouting, crowdsourcing, and public-private partnerships. Taken altogether, the introduction of these new modalities, and even more important the integration of *all* modalities, into an innovation effort is a new approach to innovation strategy. It is what creates an Open Innovation Marketplace—a collection of channels and exchanges, an innovation bazaar, where creativity and ideas can be contracted, openly sourced, or globally brainstormed. It represents what *The Economist's* Tom Standage cleverly termed "meta-innovation: innovating on how we innovate."[2]

The 1990s saw many varieties of open innovation emerge or increase. There was also a growing movement in **open source software**. Although open source software development was indeed "open to the source of the solutions," the term referred to the underlying code, the "source code," and its intent to be "open to the public," meaning not copyrighted but placed in the public domain. Thus, the novel development practice of being "open to the source of ideas" didn't actually have a name of its own. There were a few examples near the turn of the century, such as Hello Brain, InnoCentive, TopCoder, BountyQuest, and X-Prize; although, X-Prize is a not-for-profit foundation that also fits the category of prize philanthropy.

As this approach was replicated at varying levels of complexity, rapid-fire, problem solving and consulting appeared in models such as e-Lance: a website that matches freelancers and work assignments; Gerson-Lehrman, a website that says it "connects the world's leading institutions with the world's leading experts"; and later Amazon's Mechanical Turk, a website that matches software developers with businesses and entrepreneurs who want mechanical tasks done; and Google Answers, an "online knowledge market" offered by Google that enabled users to post bounties for well-researched answers to their queries.

These examples are hardly exhaustive, but you get the idea. In this climate, Jeff Howe's *Wired* article in 2006[3] introduced the term **crowdsourcing**—a descriptor that has gained considerable traction. The term has been comfortably applied to both the quick response "answers" systems and more complex endeavors, such as InnoCentive.

## Prize Philanthropy

On the not-for-profit side of the spectrum, the phrase **Prize Philanthropy** is defined as the use of donated prizes to incentivize breakthroughs perceived as having some sort of broad social or philanthropic intent. In this expanding sector, you see diversification of the widely familiar X-prize efforts—the addition of the Virgin Earth Challenge, to find means for scrubbing atmospheric carbon dioxide; the Prize4Life, a foundation focused on treatment and detection of Lou Gehrig's disease; and other examples as well. What characterizes this end of the spectrum is that the qualifying submissions are often heroic in execution and require considerable investment and likely a coalition of talents and disciplines to pull off. However, Prize Philanthropy is rapidly moving "down-scale" to seek modular, turnkey solutions that are *part* of a bigger ecology in global problem solving. These would include many independent efforts, and collaborative efforts in which existing open innovation platforms serve the needs of foundations and obviate the need for massive duplication of efforts in platform construction.

# Problem Solving Versus Question Asking

When all the world becomes "the innovation lab," how do innovation competitors compete? As pointed out by Michael Raynor and Jill Panetta in *Harvard Business Publishing's* higher education newsletter, the new basis for innovation competition shifts from controlling the prior "limiting resource" of problem solvers to the new limiting resource of question-askers.[4] In open innovation, in which resources well beyond any imaginable corporate lab are available to solve problems, solvers often respond to the innovation challenges because they perceive a commitment to manufacture, market, and make their invention available to the public. In the two parts of innovation—invention and realization—this new openness, and the ease with which it can be accessed, represents a leap forward for the "invention" part, with the commitment to "realization" being a form of currency to the inventor.

Essentially, you pay people by selling what they invent. That is, the resources an idea seeker will use to distribute and commercialize an invention is beyond the scope of many would-be inventors who will engage with an expectation of some monetary return, but also with the prospect of being "paid" by having their invention marketed or even freely distributed and thus, the ability to make a difference.

This question-based competition also redefines the role for internal corporate staff, a topic addressed in much more detail in Chapter 3, "A New Innovation Framework."

In summary, innovation strategy is not an oxymoron. Failure by an organization to own that at the highest levels is a dereliction of duty.

# Part I

Challenge Driven Innovation: How
a Marketplace of Innovation Allows
Us to Reframe the Innovation Model,
Improve Performance, and Manage Risk

# 2

## The Future of Value Creation

"The corporation as we know it, which is now 120 years old, is unlikely to survive another twenty-five years. Legally and financially, yes, but not structurally and economically."

—*Peter Drucker, 2000*[1]

## Overview

Sustaining a business is the act or continual value creation. And value creation occurs via the process of innovation, whether that's innovation in strategy, business model, products, processes, or services. This chapter walks through the rationale for why a fundamental change in the way value is created—and captured by organizations—*must* occur. You will examine, using appropriate economic theories, why the modern corporation exists in the first place; and why those same theories predict different organizational structures and different economic models for the future. The early examples of this change can serve not only to support the proposal that "change is inevitable," but also to provide some suggestion as to its form.

# Transaction Costs and Vertical Integration

Ronald Coase was a professor emeritus of economics at the University of Chicago Law School when he won the 1991 Nobel Prize in economics. The economic theories that earned him this distinction centered around a seminal paper he wrote in 1937 entitled "The Nature of the Firm."[2] The phenomenon of the corporation had been evident for several decades, and Coase was looking to explain the logic behind its existence. Marketplaces had already existed for centuries, and no doubt millennia, prior to the birth of the corporation. In a marketplace, the raw materials to make a new product are purchased right before the item, whether shoe or carriage, is crafted. The saddle maker purchases leather ready for cutting and sewing into the new desired shape. The new automobile maker could likewise purchase steel, as needed, to assemble its product.

And yet, what was later to be described as **vertical integration** was evident everywhere. Rather than rely solely upon the marketplace as a source for raw materials, corporations were "diversifying" by acquiring the businesses, from which they would have purchased goods, and manufacturing those goods in addition to the final product they created for the customer.

The explanation for vertical integration was that these businesses were growing in size and complexity and they wanted to further capture the middleman's profits. But this explanation seemed inadequate. Such an approach often proved dilutive, forcing overall profit margins to decline. According to Coase, the system property responsible for vertically integrated companies was posited to be what Coase initially called "marketing costs" and which we now call **transaction costs**. These were defined as all those expenses unrelated to the actual cost paid for the raw material and yet necessary for that material's acquisition. The automaker may have paid $1.00 a pound for the sheet steel that it acquired, but that was *not* part of the transaction costs. The transaction costs, rather, included the costs associated with searching for and identifying a suitable supplier, with evaluating the quality of that supplier's product and its capability to supply it consistently. The transaction costs included the professional labor charges associated with negotiating and authoring the supply contract. And the transaction costs included the costs associated with the enforcement of that contract and the ongoing evaluation of the quality of the purchased material.

It is not difficult to imagine that these transaction costs could readily exceed the profit margin earned by the middleman and, in some cases, might even exceed the cost of the material itself. The sum of these costs, which arguably contributed nothing to the value of the ultimate product, should, thus, be minimized. The corporation was argued to exist for the purpose of minimizing these transaction costs. If the organization were, in effect, acquiring the starting materials from itself, these costs were both minimized and controlled. Vertical integration thus occurred up to some limit of reasonableness; that is, most automobile manufacturers did not enter the mining business. That said, it was not unusual for them to enter the businesses of steel, paint, and electronics.

# Vertical Disintegration

It is interesting, in the 21st century, to reread Coase's paper. We might imagine a focus on the transaction costs associated with contract negotiation or maybe even quality control. From a modern-day perspective, it may seem that transaction costs such as search would be near trivial. But the world was a different place in 1937, and search costs were a dominant theme in Coase's work. It was just hard to find stuff. There were no Googles, yellow pages, 800-numbers, or Internet. Of course, search costs are not the only transaction costs that have dropped over the subsequent decades. Analytical automation and robotics have lowered the cost of quality inspection. Communications technologies have lowered the cost of the negotiation. Even readily available contract templates, and the ease of engaging legal firms on a purely *ad hoc* basis, reduces the costs associated with contracting. If you take Coase's work at face value, as economists have for many years and as the Nobel committee did in 1991, you must ask yourself: Would vertical integration have ever occurred to the same degree if the capabilities and technologies of the present had been available to the growing businesses of the past? And this, of course, begs a second, perhaps more relevant, question: Should you anticipate a vertical DIS-integration of old businesses, wherein marketplaces assume the role that has been played by intercorporate transfer of materials, both physical and intellectual? The answer to this second question is yes, and ironically, the organizational outcome is a different result, not for a different reason but for the very same reason. Marketplaces and exchanges will once again lower the transaction costs of doing business. Integration may have obviated the costs of search but it introduced overheads and value chain mismatches. As the ability to transact in cyberspace continues to evolve, transaction costs are driving to zero.

Both this disintegration process, and the failure of startups to integrate in the first place, is happening all around you. Yet most corporate strategies accept it in bits and pieces and do not fully account for it in their long-term planning. Compelling strategic questions would, and *should*, include the following:

- At what point in the value chain are you most capable of making a profitable contribution?
- How much more narrowly can it be defined than it has been in the past?
- What new marketplaces, and exchanges, should you engage in?
- What new ones may yet evolve, to render obsolete present-day, internal capabilities?

It should already be apparent that many of the new market exchanges will trade in intellectual rather than physical assets. For a great many businesses, and for a host of good reasons, intellectual capabilities have been jealously guarded as the "secret sauce" enabling a competitive advantage. But if and when those sauces become commodities, businesses must rethink their value proposition in addition to rethinking their organizational design in such a way that most actively taps those "idea markets."

The significance of technology in this transformation is clearly evident. And it would be tempting to assign technology a role as driver. Doing so runs the risk of overlooking an even more fundamental cause for what is going on. Although technology serves as a powerful enabler, it is, itself, a servant to social and economic pressures around the globe.

## Globalization and Competition

Thomas Friedman, in his book *The World Is Flat*, identifies three historical waves of globalization:

- **The globalization of nations:** Think British Empire at its zenith.
- **The globalization of corporations:** Think of present-day multinationals of your choosing.
- **The globalization of the individual:** A desire to reside locally while engaging globally.

At the same time, imagine the shifting values of post-baby-boom generations where lifestyle choices are as much a part of career decisions as the financial realities of survival. In this light, technological advances, such as cell phones and the Internet, enabled changes in the world of work consistent with the choices of people to engage in new ways and often at a distance. Increasingly, in the workplace, "plugging in" is replacing "showing up."

A second important driver of change is good old-fashioned business competition. With an easily searchable marketplace in specialized skills and services, individuals and small startups realize they can beat corporations at their own game—at least at their "old game." The highly integrated corporation rarely, if ever, succeeds at doing *well* all the things it does. And therein lies opportunity. "Sell the mail-room," the business adage dating back to the '60s, has expanded its targets and is now regularly encroaching upon the functions and capabilities critical to the entity's value proposition. Although divesting of the mail distribution capabilities may seem fairly obvious in today's business world, it was less so right on the heels of corporate integration. But as the mailroom and cafeterias went to contracted services, so followed packaging and printing capabilities, product manufacturing, marketing design, and so on.

For many years, some innovation functions within a corporation, such as R&D, showed a capability to resist the tendency to acquire such services externally. After all, competitive advantage in the innovation arena was seen as the most crucial to the capability to thrive in the marketplace. The last decade has shown this conventional wisdom to be neither conventional nor wise.

## Lead Users

Consider, for example, the phenomenon of lead users, ingenious consumers who provoke companies to new iterations of their products. In 2005, Eric von Hippel at MIT's Sloan School of Management published a book titled *Democratizing Innovation*.[3] In this book, von Hippel segments customers of commercial products—in particular, commercial products with a high degree of complexity and which are new to the market. One key consumer segment is a group von Hippel defined as "lead users," which are sophisticated innovators in their own right and often acquire a product as a starting material in applications where no satisfactory commercial product exists.

Lead using is not necessarily an unprecedented phenomenon. There are many similarities between a research physician who purchases a medical instrument and rewires it to detect new phenomena, for which it may not have originally been intended, and the gearhead in the 1950s who had torn apart the engine of his Mercury Coupe before it even had a chance to get dirty. What *is* new is the way in which communication technology enables you to engage with lead users and tap their ingenuity in unprecedented ways. Lead user communities can then be an important, and maybe even a dominant, source of new products for the original supplier. von Hippel's book provides tangible examples in fields as wide ranging as automotive, medicine, telecommunications, computer hardware and computer software, commercial graphics and design—it's rather difficult to imagine areas in which this lead user phenomenon is not applicable.

# Open Source Software

Bearing witness to the innovation capabilities of nonemployees, external groups, the digitization of products, and the ability of disparate contributors to work collectively through new modes of communication is the open source movement begun in the 1990s. These efforts, which led to such software products as Linux, Apache web servers, and the Perl programming language, seem to have been perfectly suited to both the new technologies and the new work patterns. The ability to migrate such distributed processes to other products is, at times, hampered by the following:

- Intellectual property protection issues
- The lack of a digital version of the task
- Middle management's reluctance to cede control to the "unruly mobs"

Nevertheless, the quality of the products produced in this manner stand as testament to what can be described as "the new normal" of distributed work and mass collaboration.

Initially, attempts were made to dismiss products produced in this manner as suitable for only the fringes, or of indeterminate quality. Time and widespread adoption appear to have rendered both criticisms moot. There were internal memos from one major software producer leaked to the Internet wherein the house engineers acknowledge the apparent high quality of these products. Although we know of no rigorous studies, it is tempting to put forth a hypothesis that software assembled without centralized guidelines might even be *more* likely devoid of systematic risks. Such risks arise where a single architectural flaw (grounded in accepted corporate norms) could creep in and cross between modules and subroutines.

As learnings from the open source movement have migrated into other products, some of the barriers mentioned earlier have been tackled, and in some cases obviated. Crowdsourcing approaches now include the ability to migrate intellectual property rights along with the ideas—for example, the InnoCentive platform. And more of the knowledge work, accompanying even highly physical innovations, is appearing online, often with emergent standards and markup languages, such as the "chemical markup language" to manage information and research centered on molecules. It can be expected that this trend will continue, enabling an ever greater openness to the innovation process. These themes and their attendant examples are examined at length in Don Tapscott and Anthony Williams's best-selling work, *Wikinomics*.[4]

# Problem Solving in Chat Rooms

Even before the current incarnation of the World Wide Web with its user-friendly interface, groups of users were banding together in USENET communities to exchange ideas, practices, fixes to faulty hardware and software, and otherwise share innovations. Chat rooms are a "wikinomical" example familiar to a great many customers and stand in stark contrast to the expert helplines of old. Questions posed within a chat room often seem to get answered more rapidly and with greater reliability than when those same questions are posed to technicians working for the product company and even specifically trained to respond to customer needs. Reasons for why this is so include issues of self-selection and experiential diversity, topics which won't be expanded on here but receive more discussion later.

## Chat Rooms Versus Expert Help Desks

I was having a great deal of difficulty fitting an older Nikon lens to a newer digital body and having it function as it should. I returned to the camera shop where the body had been purchased and asked about compatibility with that particular lens. I was assured that there should be no problem and that the two units were fully compatible. Still failing to get them to work together, I brought both into the store where the local camera experts tried as well—with unsatisfactory results. They suggested that their reference material may not be up-to-date and perhaps I should call the helpline to verify the compatibility of the body and lens.

A call to that helpline, and subsequent conversation with the expert who answered it, again produced assurances that the two parts were intended to work together. After following the troubleshooting script, and again without a successful outcome, it was suggested that I package up both the lens and body and ship it to them where they promised to give me a definitive answer within weeks—weeks that I would be without either of these items.

Although I had little experience with chat rooms at that point in time, I had little to lose—as the alternatives of accepting the products' incompatibility or waiting weeks for the problem to be resolved at the factory seemed unsatisfactory. I went online and found an appropriate forum and posed my question. I received a response within minutes along with a series of additional questions to help a fellow Nikon user troubleshoot the issue. I pulled out my camera and lens, and went through each troubleshooting question providing answers to the best of my ability. And again, within minutes, the diagnosis returned with the description of a suitable workaround enabling the lens and digital body to work as expected.

I know from watching my children that the hours I have spent in my life on "helpline-hold" will never be wasted by them. I've frequently seen them immediately drop their queries into the online forums where hundreds, possibly thousands, of experienced users stand ready to aid a fellow traveler—whether it's a software installation, a mechanical assembly, or turning off a pesky idiot light.

Chat room stories are reflected in other social media as well, such as wikis and blogs, and again testify to the capability of such tools to aggregate what might be deemed "collective intelligence," or more simply, the "wisdom of the crowd." Although this notion is discussed in Chapter 4, "The Long Tail of Expertise," the phenomenon of crowd wisdom or intelligence is not described at length for the simple reason that better analyses may be found by reading *The Wisdom of Crowds*,[5] *Wikinomics*,[6] *Social Nation*,[7] salient articles and books by Eric von Hippel, or in the impressive efforts of the Center for Collective Intelligence at MIT under the direction of Professor Thomas Malone. That is not to say that present-day study or knowledge about such phenomena is anywhere near complete, or even well documented. Indeed, it is no doubt in its infancy. This book's intent is to show how such capabilities change the game of innovation and how businesses that want to effectively compete must forge a deliberate strategy for their adoption and implementation.

## Not by Bread Alone: Diverse Utilities

One criticism leveled against such open approaches is that they seem to be inherently "second-rate" and unsustainable. After all, how can an open wiki, such as Wikipedia, ever produce articles of quality commensurate with those produced by hand-picked experts who are compensated for their work and thereby motivated to ensure the article's scholarship and accuracy.

Frequently, overlooked in these criticisms is the economic concept of mixed utilities. Economics, which has sought to rationally explain the motives behind the exchange of goods and the behavior of markets has, in some sectors, recently devolved into an analysis of monetary policy and corporate financials. In the recent global economic crisis of 2008–2010, much has been written about "the new capitalism." One characteristic feature of "the new capitalism" is that it involves more than just money. This new economic frontier suggests that people actually work and contribute for reasons other than

money, and that sometimes their choice making cannot be rationalized on a monetary basis alone. We read these things not with dis-
agreement, but amusement. The "new economics" smells a lot like
the old, old economics. In the 1700s and 1800s, utilitarian economists
such as Jeremy Bentham and John Stuart Mill, wrote of maximizing—
not cash, but—happiness. Admittedly, happiness is a far more difficult metric than dollars to plug into the latest Monte Carlo
simulations.

Dusting off both the oldest and the newest economic theories is
necessary to explain the engagement of passionate, but "unpaid,"
individuals, whether they are troubleshooting a lens compatibility
problem, blogging their perspective on health care, writing an article
on solar energy for Wikipedia, or solving a complex challenge to
improve the quality of space food posted on InnoCentive. One of several recent phenomena in innovation—but largely closed to closed
innovation—is this ability to attract many diverse motives and utilities—held by contributors who more than gladly accept payment on a
much broader basis than cash alone. Exploiting those utilities, while
not exploiting the individuals, is a crucial part of learning to organize
and work in new and unfamiliar ways.

## Count What Counts

Albert Einstein once said, "Not everything you can count counts."
To function under this new order, you not only need to organize and
work in new ways, but to change the very metrics for reporting and
judging performance—both at the corporate and individual level.
The present measurements all too often stand as outright barriers to
real progress. A simple example will help make this point: In a closed
shop, one of several measurements might be total expenses per
employee—salaries, benefits, and their consumption of materials
such as travel, paper, chemicals, and so on. The efforts of management to pay fairly, but not excessively, to avoid waste, to fully use

existing equipment (that is, not replace laptops every year) all suggest that this measurement is a number that should be *minimized*. And, as such, managers may set expense targets per employee, not to be exceeded.

Yet, in an open environment—in which each internal employee is seen as a point of leverage to multiple external contacts and ideas, each of which represents a variable and not a fixed expense—this measurement of expenses per employee should be *maximized*. Thus, a company that retains its old metrics of cost-per-employee minimization, while espousing a strategy of openness, is probably doomed to failure. Although this example serves to illustrate the often oxymoronic, and sometimes just plain moronic, conflict between old productivity metrics and new ways of working, maybe one slightly more sophisticated example is in order.

In the world of business, gross profit margin is a percentage where, simply, bigger is seen as better. It is a financial measure often sought out for comparison between corporations, within the same general sector, and another example of a number for which the simple objective of maximization is usually applied. The gross profit margin for any item is the percent of cash obtained on each sale after subtracting the cost of producing that good (many times abbreviated as COGS, costs of good sold). A $200 digital camera, may require $80 of parts and labor to assemble. The $120 is the profit representing a gross profit margin of 60%. A higher gross profit margin is usually perceived as providing greater latitude in the use of the cash (price minus COGS) for purposes of investment in future products, investment in marketing, distribution as profit to shareholders, or for capital acquisitions. Affiliates and sales forces are usually mindful that the gross margin differs from product to product, and thus that the overall corporate gross margin is enhanced by selling a disproportionately larger number of products with the smallest COGS.

Open innovation can often run afoul of this measurement because R&D investments in that product, or even ongoing improvements, are considered a sunk internal R&D expense, and that's not reflected in the COGS, resulting in exaggerated gross margins. However, externally derived products, in which the R&D investment risk occurred in a different organization, are often acquired with a royalty obligation, on sales, to be paid to the innovator, a number that is usually allocated to the COGS. Consequently, even a beneficially negotiated royalty rate can lead an affiliate, rewarded on the basis of its gross margin, to be motivated to sell the internally derived product even if it represents a net lesser value to the organization and a poorer long-term economic picture. When embarking on program of open innovation, rethink metrics and heed Einstein's advice.

# All of a Sudden

Some of the barriers discussed in this chapter serve to illustrate why there was not, and will not be, a spontaneous disintegration of the corporation under a new environment of significantly altered transaction costs. Of course, over time, the stubbornness of culture, the psychological barriers of control, the unfamiliarity of new IP terms, the incompatibilities of metrics and strategy, the masking of transaction costs as institutionalized costs of doing business, and the mixed utilities complicating both cost and return *will* get ironed out. The corporate cultures undergo their slow shifts. The bureaucracies cede to competitive realities, and regulators grudgingly yield to the pragmatic wills of consumers. In those instances, it's important to have an underlying model and understanding of the forces and drivers and the directions that they are pushing.

Recent discussions with Thomas Malone, at MIT, have found him scratching his head and wondering whether or not his crystal ball was on the fritz when, in 2004, he wrote, *The Future of Work*, predicting many of the changes described here. But changes *are* underway and we are reminded of an exchange between Hemingway characters in *The Sun Also Rises*: "How did you go bankrupt?" Bill asked. "Two ways," Mike said. "Gradually and then suddenly."[8] And so cultural change and organizational change often appears to be progressing "gradually" at first, and about the time you are ready to abandon your predictions, the change occurs "suddenly." During the gradual phase, the reality of the change is doubted by many. It's all just a matter of "waiting it out." The good old days are just around the corner. But then, suddenly, the business is gone, the opportunities are gone, and you are left wondering how so much could happen so fast. Looking again at Peter Drucker's quote, at the opening of this chapter, you can pause and do the math; it is now more than a decade old, and in many ways we don't seem much closer to his dire prediction that we were in 2000. But 10 or 15 years is more than enough time for the "all of a sudden" phase.

Change is often categorized as evolutionary or revolutionary— the first characterized generally by slowness and subtlety and the second by speed and shock. Is this shift from closed innovation to open innovation—a change that threatens to escalate the vertical disintegration of corporations—evolutionary or revolutionary? The evolutionary argument is made strongly on the basis that the selective pressures, that is, Coase's transaction costs, are still at work in shaping the emergence of new business species and the extinction of old ones.

But any established corporation that wants to transcend this change and emerge as a competitor for the future is going to have to make radical shifts in the way it organizes, the way it rewards, and in the way it measures its performance, especially in the areas of innovation. To the leaders who have dared to implement such change, at a time when things seem to be evolving slowly, it's going to feel, indeed, it is going to *be*, revolutionary.

The simple truth is: You must revolt to evolve.

# Case Study: How Orchestration Creates Value for Li and Fung

Each year it produces more than 2 billion toys, consumer items, and articles of clothing, and yet it owns not a single manufacturing facility. It stocks the shelves of many famous retail chains without a shipping department. It is responsible for the continued employment of 2 million persons around the world; and yet, only ½ of 1 percent of those carry a company ID card. Might it be some "new economy" startup, funded out of Silicon Valley, a Threadless 3.0? Actually, it has been in business not only before the Internet existed, but years before the first radio broadcasts by Charles Herrold. It is Li and Fung, founded toward the end of the Qing Dynasty, in 1906, in Guangzhou, China. It brokered trade in its early days, evolved into a Hong Kong-based exporter, and finally became a multinational corporation. In the early '80s, it examined its business model and began operating in the unusual manner that characterizes it today.

The approach used by Li and Fung has been described by John Hagel and John Seely Brown as "process orchestration."[9] The network that it "orchestrates" includes more than 8,300 suppliers located in more than 40 countries. It was among the first to ship final product labels, showing the actual retail price, direct to manufacturers, who included them with the products, and then shipped directly to the retail outlet, saving weeks over the normal processes of receiving at a wholesaler's facility, repackaging, and then finally pricing. At the time, the move was radical. Why would any intermediary choose to be so transparent about retail pricing with a supplier who might use the information to squeeze a few extra cents into its wholesale price? Of course, the information, so closely held, was available to any consumer who walked in the store. But the mentality at the time was to play that card close to the vest. However, as Li and Fung began collaborating, instead of competing, with its own supply chain, it shaved time (and cost!) off many steps of the process, much more than the few cents that might arrive in a wholesaler's hands. In all, it was a more economical process that created greater value for producers, middlemen, and of course, Li and Fung.

Victor and William Fung, along with Jerry Wind, of the Wharton School, captured the elements of its success in the book *Competing in a Flat World: Building Enterprises for a Borderless World*. Therein they say, "What the discipline of management was to the old vertically integrated, hierarchical firm, network orchestration is to the company working in the flat world. It is an essential capability for this world, from orchestrating virtual networks such as Wikipedia and open-source software to delivering hard goods through global manufacturing,"[10] and "The movement from a traditional firm toward network orchestrator requires a shift in focus from the firm to the network, a shift in management from control to empowerment, and a shift in value creation from specialization to integration."[11] The reality is that the management skills practiced, honed, and rewarded for decades don't prepare current executives for the shift to the role of orchestrator. And yet it does not lie entirely outside of their grasp, as illustrated by Li and Fung's long history and deep, cultural traditions prior to its transformation.

John Hagel, Scott Durchslag, and John Seely Brown identify three key steps in a migration path from a traditionally managed firm to a more effective entity employing the art of orchestration: 1) orchestration skill-building, 2) self orchestration, and 3) process network orchestration.[12] It is unlikely that these steps will be undertaken and effectively completed without deliberate decisions by senior management. Senior managers must recognize that their mandate to create value applies not only to the present but also to the future, in which the world becomes increasingly flatter. The time to begin building the organization's orchestration skills is now.

Even in the most carefully vertically integrated corporation, there will exist supply and value chain mismatches in scale. It is these mismatches that create the opportunity to use those newly acquired orchestration skills to more loosely couple the value chain segments. In other words, allow downstream components to access supply from external sources and internal ones. Compete even. Is the external product outperforming in features, quality, or price? You can recouple the value chain and force your company to use its inferior, internally derived product. But where's the wisdom in that? And further, allow upstream components to overproduce in circumstances when they can gather value by supplying external users with their product. Taking these steps in the near term can help an executive team prepare for the longer term.

# 3

# A New Innovation Framework

"The boundaries between the firm and its environment have become more permeable."

—*Wikipedia on Open Innovation*

## Overview

Current employment strategies usually rely on some rational compromise between hiring people with skills that are needed immediately and hiring people with skills that will likely be needed in the future. A more open approach to innovation promises access to "smart people" that are outside of your organization. But most strategies fall far short of effectively tapping that external crowd. A new framework for innovation should position leaders to understand both *why* and *how* to extract value external to their organization. A framework will be posited in lieu of the traditional innovation approach of stage-gate management. That new framework is designed to subdivide projects into modules, not stages—modules that are more amenable to sharing within a network of resources and among a variety of innovation approaches.

The human resources department, along with the innovation functions, in a company practicing Challenge Driven Innovation recognizes their broader role in accessing talent. They realize that effective management of this resource involves *both* internal and external persons that can effectively contribute. They appreciate the fact that internal experts better understand the nature of the problem or need, that they comprehend "local" limitations and implementation concerns. But they also know that many times the best minds for a given task lie outside the walls of the organization and they know the most appropriate mechanisms to find, enroll, and use those resources.

# Open Innovation's Unique Potential

Arguments for open innovation often seem to hinge upon sentiments similar to those once expressed by technology investor Bill Joy of Sun Microsystems: "Most of the smart people work for someone else." You can certainly agree to the truthfulness of this declaration. Most of the people a company would label "smart," do work somewhere else. But this simple observation does not provide any guidance on what to do about that fact. Rather, you should ask the question, "What does the practice of open innovation, the tapping of smart people who don't work for you, do for your business that closed innovation cannot?" Answers to that question would likely start with arguments for how open innovation better manages diversity and risk sharing.

Recall Damon Runyon's comments that opened the first chapter: "The race is not always to the swift nor the battle to the strong, but that's the way to bet." For most organizations, the act of hiring is an act of betting, and the smart money will be the selection of "the swift and the strong." In a business hiring case, "swift" and "strong" are interpreted in the context of the skills and disciplines being sought. You want to recruit and hire the strongest lawyer, the swiftest chemical engineer, and the strongest C++ programmer you can find.

But Runyon correctly argues that the race might be won otherwise. And history shows its complete support for that contention. Was it not an Augustinian monk, Gregor Mendel, who laid the foundations of genetics? Was it not an academically unemployable patent clerk, Albert Einstein, who shredded all assumptions about space time? Was it not a bookseller's apprentice, Michael Faraday, who discovered many of the elements of electromagnetism? No one is disputing the raw intellect of these contributors. One is merely acknowledging the likelihood that they all would have failed the employment criteria in biology, cosmology, and telecommunications, respectively, even just before their seminal breakthroughs. In many cases, in a highly specialized world, someone from another discipline, such as a physicist solving a biochemistry problem, is the one who grabs the brass ring, or wins the race.

Yet, the hinted-at, alternative employee recruitment strategy is completely untenable. Yes, the heat exchanger problem in a production plant *might* be best solved, not by a chemical engineer, but by a residential furnace technician, an automobile repair man, or a computer chip designer—or for that matter, an archaeologist, a veterinarian, or a maid. But so what? Surely there is no intention to hire all six of these individuals...just in case. And even less intention of hiring the other 60 qualifications who *might* have been speculated on in this paragraph. To do so would be an act of lunacy. Enter open innovation.

The merit of accessing talent from outside the prevailing disciplines is recognized. Stan Davis and Chris Meyer, in their book *Blur*, suggest as one of "50 ways to blur your business" that you challenge the proclivity of Ivy League groupthink by hiring a "trade school grad with a guitar and a tattoo."[1] But, of course, capriciously hiring an "unqualified" cadre would be an abuse of resources. On the other hand, contracting with them may indeed offer some viable alternatives. And this latter approach holds an even greater likelihood of a favorable outcome if this work, or their contributions to it, could be done in parallel, with value assigned to the contribution only *after* the fact. Could that heat exchanger problem have been worked on simultaneously by the chemical engineer, the furnace technician, the auto repairman, AND the chip designer? And, after the fact, could the heat exchanger owner have reviewed the results and elected to pay for outcomes as opposed to efforts? Suddenly a "guitarist with a tat-too" is not only a challenge to our way of thinking but a viable way to *actually* get creative work done.

In this scenario, you can see the role open innovation potentially plays in both diversity and risk-sharing: The contributors assume the risk that their contribution may not be deserving of post-facto com-pensation commensurate with the effort undertaken. If this were the only way open innovation was designed to work, it would probably fail. But risk-sharing business models that provide access to diversity and self-selection mechanisms enable many of these benefits to be achieved in a fair and equitable environment. So much so, that any organization that relies exclusively on the employment mechanism for accessing talent is guilty of under-serving its stakeholders.

## A Rational Compromise

It was this central constraint of employment "bets"—the limita-tion that closed innovation was performed by those that had been interviewed, selected, and recruited even before the task was known—that led Eli Lilly to its original founding of InnoCentive and other open innovation systems. Lilly wanted access to a greater diver-sity of approaches than it made sense to acquire through hiring the many, many new employees that would have created that diversity internally.

Many times the work to be carried out in an industrial setting is unlike any specific work an employee has ever done before. How then is qualification determined in order for work to be appropriately assigned? It is usually done on the basis of broad skill sets. That is to say that computer programmers are assigned to learn and write in a new language. MBAs are assigned to manage something they've never managed before. Solid state physicists are asked to invent bet-ter hard drive materials. And marketers are asked to develop cam-paigns for products they only just discovered even existed. All of these are somewhat non-ideal. The employees assigned are roughly, but not ideally, qualified. They are what might be referred to a rational compromise.

# Exploring Problem-Solving Diversity

Consider instead the well-publicized story of Goldcorp. Goldcorp owned mining rights on about 55,000 acres near Red Lake in Northern Ontario. The founder and chairman at the time, Rob McEwen had listened to the many perspectives on how and where the gold might be found in greater quantities, yielding a higher overall mine productivity. While Rob understood that a deep geological science lay at the root of these conclusions, the variables were never perfectly controlled and the conclusions were based on assumptions and models as much a part of tradition as they were of rigorous objectivity. McEwen wanted to take a new tact. He proposed that the geological survey data be freely given to anyone seeking it in exchange for their hypotheses on where gold might be more prevalent. To the person(s) providing the answer that best panned out for Goldcorp's efforts, they would award $575,000 in prize money. The survey data was shared with over 1,000 groups and individuals who were interested in tackling the effort. Proposals came from all around the world and from many individuals outside the mining industry, and certainly from many who were not even trained geologists. The winning entry was a collaborative effort by two groups from Australia: Fractal Graphics, in West Perth, and Taylor Wall & Associates, in Queensland. The graphic methods they employed provided an entirely new perception of the data and lead the Red Lake mine to become the most productive gold mine in history.

Most innovation leaders appreciate that, for sufficiently complex problems—as most of the interesting ones are—"solution space," the matrix of all possible solutions, is usually too vast for a complete search. But, none of that suggests that innovation can't be much better than it is—that it can't be greatly improved with a new approach.

It's that potential for improvement—evident in the contrast between what was produced via the Goldcorp approach and what gets produced under classical, serial, commercial assignments—that suggests the need for a new innovation framework and mechanism for rationally engaging in open innovation. A greater diversity of approaches to problems in commercial, philanthropic, or government endeavors would likely yield superior solutions, greater economic viability, and shorter innovation cycles—all of which would ultimately benefit both shareholders and customers. These are the issues that presently drive the adoption of open innovation by the most successful innovators.

# Risk Sharing

As previously stated, open innovation can do (at least) *two* things that closed innovation cannot. The first is to effectively exploit diversity, and the second is to share risk. The point has been made of the manner in which open innovation enables the effectiveness of greater diversity. This important topic is one we will continue probing in Chapter 4, "The Long Tail of Expertise." At this juncture, a bit more should be said about the sharing of risk. It is beyond the intended scope of the book to go into great detail about the complex subject of risk management. But, as mentioned in the introductory chapter, within the innovation endeavor, risk rears its head in the form of: financial risk, having to pay for things before success is assured; technical risk, some ideas don't actually work; and execution risk, it would have worked, but the endeavor was done ineffectively.

In a closed innovation system, all of these risks are borne *solely* by the innovating organization. It must pay for projects whether they ultimately succeed or fail. In an open innovation system, these risks may be shared with partners enabling their more effective management and permitting risky portfolios to be increased in size—the same budget will pay *half* the costs for *twice* as many projects—providing diversification and lowering the risk of the portfolio yielding an excessive number of failures.

Even more significant than simply the sharing of risk is the observation that risk itself is asymmetrical. That is, the amount of risk offloaded by one party may be considerably greater than the amount of risk the other party assumes.

In the incubation phase of InnoCentive, some pointed out that the assumption of risk by the solver community was unsustainable. The solvers, collectively, would not, and could not, continue to experiment at their own risk, especially not on behalf of a well-funded and successful commercial entity. At some point, economic speculation goes, it had to all balance out and you couldn't get any more risk-taking out the system than was commensurate with the return that was available. It didn't really matter who the participants were, internal or external, but the asymmetry of risk, fueled by non-cash utilities, effectively obviates this concern and allows a network to assume more risk than the expected return would predict. Let's be more specific.

The likelihood for solver engagement was assessed during a prelaunch roadshow, as the founders met with various potential solvers. During a meeting with Professor Tom Wandless at Stanford University, the overall idea was outlined, and Professor Wandless was asked if he might, under *any* circumstances, be willing to participate. His response was that he had grave doubts about whether he would ever even *consider* altering his research endeavors in response to a posted challenge. But, he then added that one of his ongoing research interests was the design of new synthetic routes to dehydroamino acids. He said that if one of the posted challenges needed such an effort, he might be willing to "put their compound in my table." By this he meant that he would consider adding an example to a table of examples in the work he was already doing. He added that, if a bounty *was* posted for the solution, he would be willing to cash the check. He was saying that a posted challenge, looking for new ways to make dehydroamino acids was work he would be undertaking anyway, and it would be of little inconvenience to add to his efforts the specific research that the challenge-posting company was "off-loading." In essence, you aren't taking on more risk if you were going to do the work (or something closely akin to it) anyway.

A second way in which the off-loaded risk is of different magnitude than the assumed risk by individual solvers is related to the assignment process. The risk of innovating in a corporate setting must take into account the issue raised earlier: that task allocation is inefficient and involves compromises—compromises that raise the financial risk as failures accumulate and raise the execution risk as non-ideal executors contribute to false negative conclusions. In some open models, the persons tackling the problem self-select which helps further obviate the non-ideal assignment of tasks. For these reasons and others, individual researchers and small contract firms are often more than willing to accept some risk and work without a *guarantee* of payment. This creates innovation opportunities via external efforts that are simply *impossible* with closed innovation approaches alone.

## Innovation Marketplaces

Given the posited strong advantages of open innovation in diversity and risk sharing, why is the vast majority of ongoing corporate research still carried out internally? It is a question delved into more deeply later in the book. Setting aside, for the moment, the substantial issues of cultural change and institutionalized processes, one significant factor is simply closed innovation's ready availability: because it's there. Historically, open innovation projects have been prefaced by the need to locate a partner, to negotiate with that partner, and to transfer existing know-how—the very transaction costs that hold corporations in place and which were discussed in the preceding chapter. The new business models and "innovation marketplaces" are lowering those costs and creating an environment in which open innovation will soon dominate. They are doing this by better search procedures, templated agreements, intellectual property commons (where people freely give away their know-how without charge), and intellectual assets and commodity exchanges. Bear in mind that in a connected world, many things are potentially commodities that were specialized contracts in the past—for example, Internet bandwidth, novel molecules, or logo designs. In the process, these changes—and exchanges—are creating new and unfamiliar roles for the internal researchers, technologists, designers, and innovators—new roles that will also call for a new process framework for innovation.

## Historical Stage-Gate Processes

This global market and capabilities shift prompts speculation as to how an organization's innovation framework and processes may evolve in accord with these broad changes. The current dominant paradigm for internal innovation is the **stage-gate process**. Closed innovation is an inherently serial process. (You try and fail, and try again, until it is good enough, or you abandon the effort.) As this process has been subjected to the scrutiny of corporate efficiency, it has been architected as a linear and ordered sequence of major stages separated by gates. The gates are usually characterized by performance criteria used to determine a project's readiness to enter the next stage, or precipitate a termination decision. These periodic checkpoints serve to elicit conscious decisions from the organization, and give attention to project performance, to minimize wasteful spending on false positives and to ensure that successful projects, clearing the last stage and launched into the marketplace, will perform as expected and with appropriate returns on the research investment.

Depending on the sector, and actually, even the individual project, the stages and gates through which the project travels may differ slightly. For a typical circumstance, imagine five stages and four gates, with the final gate being the project's admission into production and the marketplace. Although the words will frequently differ, a representative series of stages might be perceived as: idea, validation, proof of concept, prototype, and production. This arrangement is well-suited for an internal, serial process, with gate point checks and balances on viability and returns, and will undoubtedly survive to some degree even as open innovation is more fully exploited.

Alone, the stage-gate process fails to either effectively manage or fully capture the opportunities presented via "full" innovation: open plus closed. In an environment where both modes of innovation are practiced, would this stage-gate mechanism still dominate? After all, open innovation can be decidedly parallel, and that is a feature that *should* be exploited. Stages and gates manage cost containment by setting gate criteria such that projects that become too risky, too likely to fail, are terminated before more money is spent on their development. But in open innovation, when those high-risk costs are assumed, or at least shared, by others, it is less critical that termination criteria be prematurely applied by passing through frequent gates or decision points.

Although one would never argue for throwing out some of the distinctive benefits of the stage-gate paradigm, you might argue for its cohabitation alongside other project paradigms to organize the open innovation process. The alternative framework put forward at this time is **Challenge Driven Innovation, CDI**, which shares DNA with the modularity processes, earlier described by Carliss Baldwin and Kim Clark of Harvard Business School.[2] In CDI, a portion of the larger project is formulated as a challenge, in which a "challenge" essentially represents the problem statement for a block of work that can be modularized and in most cases rendered "portable." That is, such a block of work can be outsourced or insourced as an integral unit. The central processes to this framework are those of dissection, channel distribution, and integration. The remainder of this chapter describes this methodology and its implication for redefining the organization focused on innovation, and most specifically for redefining the internal skill sets and tasks that have to be altered in the post-open world. This section wraps up with a hypothetical example from the world of medicines development along with real-world examples consistent with this approach.

# Seven Stages of Challenge Driven Innovation

Because the stage gate framework is so generalizable, it might be tempting to read the following as nothing more than a renaming of the stages. Try not to do so. These may be overlapping and iterate. But most important, the activities generally associated with the stage-gate mechanism are almost entirely conducted between activities number 4 and number 5, where the default channel is to conduct the work internally.

1. *Idea gathering:* The open front-end of the innovation development funnel. It is the gathering of more opportunities than you have the capacity to manage so that the most promising can be selected for moving forward.

2. *Filtering:* The selection of projects best-suited to development and marketing by your organization. The culling of projects that either fail to meet targeted returns or do not fit strategically with corporate objectives.

3. *Dissection:* The decomposition of a large, complex project into discrete modules. These modules are larger than individual tasks but considerably smaller than the overall project itself. They are of a scale and properties that can be made modular in the sense described by Baldwin and Clark (referenced earlier); that is, they can be executed according to recipe or end product specifications. They can be made portable and placed as an

integral body of work to be executed either internally or externally. Each of these modules of an innovation can be characterized as a problem statement or "challenge."

4. ***Channel distribution:*** The placement of the above work units, or challenges, into the appropriate innovation channels. Innovation channels include, but are not limited to, contract research organizations, academic projects and grants, joint ventures, and of course, internal efforts. Much more will be said about these channels and how to select them in Chapter 5, "The Selection of Appropriate Innovation Channels."

5. ***Evaluation/confirmation:*** The receipt of the completed challenge modules from the channels to which they were distributed, and the comparison of results against specifications and performance criteria.

6. ***Assembly and integration:*** The reassembly of the individual challenge modules into a functional whole that is ready for market.

7. ***Launch:*** The launch of the new product, concept, or service into the market place.

The schematic in Figure 3.1 illustrates the central portion of this framework, namely: dissection; channel distribution; and evaluation and assembly.

Idea gathering is not so much the act of looking for ways to tackle a specific project, but rather an ongoing collection of what the projects or products might be that should enter the innovation framework. Filtering is simply the rejection of some of those ideas based on how well or poorly they fit with the organization's core mission, or lack of adequate market interest to justify the effort. Projects that passed through the filter are then dissected, that is, broken into subprojects—a subproject being a collection of work, larger than a single task, but considerably smaller than the overall project.

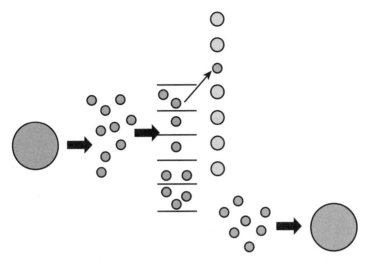

**Figure 3.1 Dissecting a large project, distributing sub-projects into appropriate innovation channels and reassembling the completed and evaluated segments into a whole for market launch.**

Channel distribution involves the selection of an appropriate innovation path for each of these subprojects, the introduction of the subproject into that channel, and the monitoring of progress. Chapter 5 discusses each of ten distinct innovation channels and the criteria by which they would be selected. Appropriate channel selection is critical to making the CDI framework effective, given the distinct qualities of the various open innovation channels available. Even with ten specific channels identified, it is still possible to mix and match and independently select funding mechanisms such that the choices grow combinatorially. The scope of possibilities has been constrained in both this chapter and Chapter 5 for the sake of a clear discussion.

Evaluation/confirmation is an activity associated with the receipt of the work product from one of the innovation paths or channels. It may be that the channel selected produces multiple options or ones that may need some adaptation. During assembly, options are selected, and the subprojects from the innovation channels are integrated as a complete project. And finally, each assembled project is launched into production and the marketplace.

It is hard to point to a good example of an entire innovation port-folio, being developed and managed like the one being described. However, the individual elements are more than evident in current organizational strategies, such as Li & Fung's "orchestration" (see the case study in Chapter 2, "The Future of Value Creation"), Procter and Gamble's "Connect and Develop" (see the case study in Chapter 6, "The Challenge Driven Enterprise"), Eli Lilly's "FIPNet" (see the case study in Chapter 5), or Prize4Life's approach to Lou Gehrig's disease (see the case study in Chapter 8, "The Challenge Driven Enterprise Playbook"). Furthermore, some examples employing elements of this innovation approach are cited and discussed later in this chapter.

## The Future of Work and the Workplace

In 1999, Stan Davis and Christopher Meyer authored *Blur: The Speed of Change in the Connected Economy*.[3] Yes, it's true the busi-ness world was abuzz with the concept of new business models. But few pundits could ground this change in the business practices and strategies of the staid brick and mortar industries that had dominated for decades. Oh sure, you had quips like "clicks and mortar," but most of the discussion centered on who'd win: Amazon or Barnes and Noble? While conceding that the world of manufacturing and supply chains might buy differently, through online exchanges, many execu-tive suites also felt a certain kind of immunity from the craziness. Was "eBay" going to produce automobiles, or was it going to discover new medicines? Davis and Meyer argued that the changes were deep and were going to touch business in many ways. It's a shame that the sub-sequent "dot-bomb" served to reinforce these executive biases of immunity. Since those days of wild swings in the NASDAQ, a lot of rethinking has been done and the implications of connection may be just as profound as originally advertised, with no natural business immunities to be found.

In their book, *Competing in a Flat World*, authors Victor Fung, William Fung, and Jerry Wind speak generally of the dissolution of corporate walls. Their comments apply across all organizational ties and include those activities associated with innovation. The authors state, "What the discipline of management was to the old vertically integrated, hierarchical firm, network orchestration is to the company working in the flat world. It is an essential capability for this world, from orchestrating virtual networks such as Wikipedia and open-source software to delivering hard goods through global manufacturing."[4]

The drivers for this change are not only organizations seeking greater efficiency; there is also a push-pull dynamic involving the desire of individuals to engage globally while maintaining their present local residence. In his book, *The World Is Flat*, Thomas Friedman calls this social phenomenon, "Globalization 3.0," and describes it as follows, "...around the year 2000 we entered a whole new era: Globalization 3.0. Globalization 3.0 is shrinking the world from a size small to a size tiny and flattening the playing field at the same time. And while the dynamic force in Globalization 1.0 was countries globalizing, and the dynamic force in Globalization 2.0 was companies globalizing, the dynamic force in Globalization 3.0—the thing that gives it its unique character—is the newfound power for individuals to collaborate and compete globally."[5] This dynamic social force is operating independently of the organizational strategies of your firm. It would be ignored at your ultimate peril.

In addition to the social *push* of Globalization 3.0, and the *pull* strategies of orchestration, the transformation underway is further assisted by technological advances. According to a monograph published by Harlan Cleveland and Garry Jacobs for the World Academy of Art & Science: "Everywhere in the world, in varying ways, information science and information technologies are accelerating the pace of change and rendering unusable familiar methods of organizing and governing that were developed for societies with clearer boundaries, more limited information flows, more stability and predictability."[6] MIT Sloan School of Management professor Thomas Malone summarized these changes in his book, *The Future of Work*.

Malone says, "...we are in the early stages of another revolution—a revolution in business—that may ultimately be as profound as the democratic revolution in government... New information technologies make this revolution possible. Dispersed physically but connected by technology, workers are now able, on a scale never before even imaginable, to make their own decisions using information gathered from many other people and places... For the first time in history, technologies allow us to gain the economic benefits of large organizations, like economies of scale and knowledge, without giving up the human benefits of small ones, like freedom, creativity, motivation, and flexibility."[7]

Without a clear example of a present-day ideal (although ALL the pieces are currently present in the business ecology), it is necessary, to hypothesize just what such a future innovation entity might look like. For purposes of contrast, the present state of predominantly closed innovation is described and then the points of difference are highlighted.

# Innovation Tasks: Internal and External

Using the familiar 80/20 rule, you could say that present day commercial innovation is carried out with an estimated 80 percent internal resources and 20 percent external ones. As it actually turns out, this is a bit of an exaggeration in favor of external activity. In 2003, the percentage of R&D work carried out externally was reported by the National Science Foundation as only 5 percent.[8] In the subsequent five years years, that number essentially doubled to 12 percent.[9] Few leaders engaged in innovation will have any reason to doubt either that magnitude nor the direction of change. The vast majority of innovation work is still carried out internally; but, you can see a steady increase in the use of external or open innovation approaches. To further understand this internal/external split and to contrast it with a proposed future state, you need to also look at what the typical activities are, for both the 88 percent spent internally and the 12 percent of innovation budgets spent externally. (It should be noted that the actual percentages reported by the NSF are skewed slightly upward by the pharmaceutical industry, which owns a fairly large proportion of the national R&D budget, roughly 20%, and which conducts clinical trials at academic and other external research centers comprising about 25% of their total R&D budget. This is pointed out in the second NSF report referenced.)

These R&D-specific figures are useful to gain some perspective—and the emerging market capability measured in hundreds of billions is worth at least some attention from corporate leadership across the pertinent sectors. But, recognize that there are many innovation activities not captured by the NSF fractions. Some functional areas, charged with innovation, may make virtually no use of open innovation—while others, like marketing have a long history of using external talent agencies to build innovative marketing campaigns.

Breaking these internal/external figures down further, the internal innovation activities consist predominantly of what is designated "data generation," as this is the dominant activity of most research or innovation endeavors, whether they are basic in nature, late-stage product oriented of even the time-consuming activities of iterative design testing or focus group conduction and evaluation. This is probably two-thirds of the time and dollars spent internally. A smaller fraction is given to hypothesis or idea generation, and the remainder to the design of studies and experiments, and to overall project coordination. Although the numbers are meant to be estimates, and account for a wide range of sectors and objectives, some more detailed suggestions for how this activity is distributed are shown in Figure 3.2. The external innovation effort is presently focused primarily on overflow data generation—work beyond the company's capacity to handle—which Figure 3.2 refers to as "scaling data generation." And a smaller, but likely substantial, portion of external innovation is to access skills, tools, and resources not available internally.

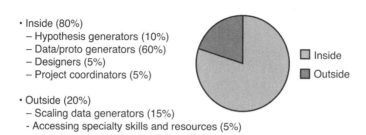

• Inside (80%)
  – Hypothesis generators (10%)
  – Data/proto generators (60%)
  – Designers (5%)
  – Project coordinators (5%)

• Outside (20%)
  – Scaling data generators (15%)
  - Accessing specialty skills and resources (5%)

☐ Inside
☐ Outside

**Figure 3.2    Present day division of innovation activities between internal and external resources.**

In the new innovation framework discussed, this 80/20 distribution of activities flips and becomes a 20/80 distribution, with 80 percent of the effort carried out *externally*, as shown in Figure 3.3. A key point to note, in comparing Figures 3.2 and 3.3, is the change in skills required for the internal effort in a more open innovation model. Internally, much of the work consists of monitoring and evaluating those activities placed externally into appropriate innovation channels. It also requires skills in project dissection, channel orchestration, and reassembly—skills generally not demanded within a closed innovation world and for which training is lagging. As before, a substantial amount of the overall effort is expended on data and prototype generation. But this work is almost exclusively the province of external innovation. The judgment-based activities of hypothesis generation and design are also performed predominantly externally. This enables the innovation orchestrator to tap the diversity of the external world to generate design and hypothesis *options*, which are then evaluated and selected by internal personnel.

The radical change suggested for internal innovation capabilities is going to be met by substantial barriers. It is for this reason that you might be tempted to observe that it may be newly created organizations, or not-for-profit endeavors, that first manifest the full implementation. After all, they typically have much smaller internal staffs who are anchored—and more importantly already successful—in historical practices. In fact, the greater resistance can be expected by the best of performers; they *succeeded* in an old framework, why risk changing that?

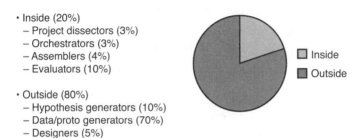

• Inside (20%)
  – Project dissectors (3%)
  – Orchestrators (3%)
  – Assemblers (4%)
  – Evaluators (10%)

• Outside (80%)
  – Hypothesis generators (10%)
  – Data/proto generators (70%)
  – Designers (5%)

■ Inside
■ Outside

**Figure 3.3    Future division of innovation activities between internal and external resources.**

# Not-for-Profit Organizations

With a growing innovation marketplace, it is easy to imagine that for some special health-care sectors, the not-for-profit model might conceivably succeed commercial entities by introducing and delivering certain goods and services under more globally affordable and sustainable conditions. This application of open innovation is already being proved out in neglected diseases, as we will see in the examples that follow and the Prize4Life case study at the end of Chapter 8. Foundations have, to a greater degree, acted as "orchestrators" versus their commercial counterparts, which most often cast themselves in the role of "doer." Historically, many not-for-profit foundations have seen their role, through orchestrating, as primarily stimulator and educator rather than producer. In today's world, those orchestrating foundations have the capability to locate the innovation and production tools to convert intention to actual products and then exploit openly sourced supply chains to deliver final products to those in need.

Ultimately, the for-profit versus not-for-profit distinction is a bit contrived. Both economic models reside on a spectrum of means for acquiring operating capital. When viewed this way, it is easy to imagine that ultimate success in an open framework will reside in mixed utility models, which employ a combination of capital sources, both philanthropic, through donations, and commercial, through sales. A lengthy discussion of the mixed-utility model lies outside this book's scope. But it is hoped that not-for-profit organizations are attending to the organizational transformation, contained in this text, with the same attention as their commercial counterparts. It is also hoped that not-for-profits recognize the role that non-cash utilities play in facilitating risk-sharing in the open innovation model. Not-for-profits are frankly better positioned for several reasons, to immediately capture this motivation, and the fruits of it, in the near future.

# Open Medicines Development: Early Steps

Although much of the foregoing may feel a bit abstract, this discussion of a new, open, innovation framework finishes by creating a simple example. The example is drawn from the sector that often lives on the boundary between commercial and philanthropic activities, even today—that is, the discovery and development of new medicines for diseases around the globe. While taking no issue with the success or motives that have driven the advancement of medicine by commercial entities, it is still recognized that some nations (and their populations) lack the economic resources to pay for the treatments that might be effective against the diseases that most often claim their citizen's lives. And even in well-developed economies, rare diseases receive less attention from large commercial organizations. This is because the struggle to develop medicines for these diseases require no less investment or effort, while the absence of a large, wealthy market for these drugs effectively *ensures* a lesser return. For these reasons, for-profits and not-for-profits have existed side-by-side in the world of medicines for the past century. If ever there were a sector ripe for a more open innovation model, and the mixed-utility entity, it is hard to imagine one better suited.

Pharmaceutical research is one of the best-funded research programs on the planet. And yet a seeming paradox exists. Funding for this research by the United States federal government exceeds $50 billion per year, and allowing for inflation, it has persisted at high levels for decades. Without question, some of the finest minds in this technical discipline reside in government research labs and academic posts throughout the world. And yet, even by analysis of the funders themselves, this enormous noncommercial effort brings few drugs directly to the taxpayers who fund it. That is not to say that the fundamental research studies carried out in these laboratories are not of enormous value in laying the technological framework for the discovery of medicines and their development primarily by commercial entities. The point is not that taxpayer dollars are wasted. Rather, the nature of the tasks, their careful integration, and the divergent cultures of basic and applied research, led to a dominating commercial corporate form that, for all the reasons discussed in Chapter 2—the management of transaction costs—historically yielded the most productive engine. But in an era of low-cost search, online collaboration, electronic transactions, and global engagement, those same forces are likely to yield a different organizational structure.

Put simply: If good science was all it took, Harvard would already be the world's most successful drug company. But diseases need pharmacological hypotheses; they need biological models; they need lead molecules; they need structure activity relationship studies, and much more. The drug candidates that spring from such early studies need analytical methods; they need efficacious formulations; they need manufacturing processes; and again, much more. The end products, the medicines that show safety and efficacy, need production facilities, quality assurance, and an efficient supply chain to reach patients around the world. Could this enormous spectrum of activity be carried out in a government, academic, or a not-for-profit organization as readily as it is in a commercial firm? Historically, probably not. But in today's connected economy, in the Open Innovation Marketplace...?

The innovation framework discussed in this chapter could bring effective medicine producing capability within the realm of all these institutional structures: government, commercial, and non-profit. That is not to say that they would *choose* to do so, but that the orchestration of innovation through dissection-channel-assembly does substantially lower the barrier to entry. Lower barriers typically bring a greater diversity of approaches, in this case ultimately resulting in new treatments and lower costs. A couple of unusual examples have already emerged.

The first is the uniquely governmental role of national defense as applied to therapeutic countermeasures for biological warfare attacks. Accept for now that the difference between treating a naturally occurring disease and one delivered by "weaponization" of infectious agents is subtle at best. "Biological warfare countermeasures" are "medicines." When these efforts were substantially refreshed following the events of 9/11, and the subsequent anthrax scare, new websites were created by the National Institute of Allergy and Infectious Disease, NIAID, that managed the product development portfolio in an unprecedentedly transparent manner. The development of these countermeasures, orchestrated by the federal government, involved the open disclosure and management of this research, and the specific stage it was in, via a public website. It might be suggested that the effectiveness of this approach was probably hampered by the attempts to shoehorn the work into classic stage-gate paradigms. Further, insufficient effort was made to redefine the orchestration, dissection, etc., skill sets and roles of those who served to advance the therapies within the NIAID. In spite of possible criticisms, the "drug development portfolio" of countermeasures was openly disclosed and enabled specialized researchers to readily assess the "state of the art" of any given countermeasure, and to independently determine how they might potentially contribute. In recent years, there seems to have been a decision to retreat from this open public view of progress. The pages, where the countermeasure projects immediate status were disclosed, have been deleted and the original URLs are redirected to web pages talking in broader generalities. Nevertheless such early efforts are commended and stand in stark contrast to the secrecy with which drug development portfolios are usually guarded.

A second example, of early efforts by noncommercial entities for the orchestration of therapeutic development, is a foundation known as "Nathan's Battle." This foundation was established by the parents and friends of a young boy, Nathan, suffering from a rare, fatal, neurodegenerative disorder known as Battens Disease. Nathan's parents come from a small business family outside the pharmaceutical industry. But, they have become sufficiently knowledgeable, with the aid of advisers, to try to tackle a problem of this magnitude through online solicitation and orchestration of the effort of others.

A portion of the Nathan's Battle website lists scientific and clinical efforts, and solicits specific needs that would enable the foundation to continue progressing the studies. When last checked, some specific needs included: "...a Good Manufacturing Practices facility to produce clinical grade virus vector for us to be used in the toxicity testing and in the clinical trial," "...a hospital to host our clinical trial as the center for the inter cranial injections and clinical evaluations. Stanford has tentatively committed to be a potential site but the FDA would like for us to have at least two sites to eliminate any bias in the test results," and "...anyone involved in these fields (enzyme replacement, gene therapy, stem cell therapy, Neurotrophic factors)." The "call to arms" ends with this statement: "At this point who you know makes a huge difference. Remember we are all just six people from everyone."[10] Not only are they using the crowd, but they're using the crowd to search the crowd.

In the coming years, these early examples will pale. Already, there are not-for-profit organizations such as the Myelin Repair Foundation and the Institute for OneWorld Health building research capabilities that rival commercial pharmaceutical companies and managing their portfolios with a new public transparency. We see open innovation efforts such as Lilly's FIPNet (see the case at end of

Chaper 5, "The Selection of Appropriate Innovation Channels") or the "Chorus model"[11] for tapping in to external resources for clinical designs at both the project and study level. There are collaborative efforts to identify malaria and tuberculosis treatments through the online sharing of data via Collaborative Drug Discovery. And the authors are aware of many more technologies, capabilities, and not-yet-public startups pursuing the discovery and development of new medicines via orchestration of the global network of research, patient advocacy, and clinical experiences.

Considering the potential that exists, these early examples may all be correctly viewed as "baby steps" but are as crucial to winning the marathon as any world-class runner's first hesitant steps were.

# Case Study: How NASA Expanded Its Innovation Framework to Find New Solutions to Old Problems[12]

A radio frequency engineer from rural New Hampshire contributed the best solution to a public challenge issued by NASA's Space Life Sciences Directorate. This is a clear example of what Aneesh Chopra, Federal Chief Technology Officer, describes as "...a notion that in our society, knowledge is widely dispersed. And if knowledge is widely dispersed, how do we capture the insights from the American people?"

Chopra also said, in the speech titled *"Rethinking Government,"* to a live audience at the 2010 Personal Democracy Forum, "A semi-retired radio frequency engineer living in rural New Hampshire was able to share his idea on how to address this problem, and it so blew away the others whose ideas were under consideration that NASA reported it exceeded their requirements! No complicated RFP, the need for lobbyists, some convoluted processes, etc. Just a smart person... (who) was paid a modest $30,000 for his insight."[13]

In 2005, NASA had to make choices about how to support the Constellation Program, an ambitious program to take humans back to the moon for months at a time. It was designed eventually to take people to Mars, on missions longer than two years, requiring unprecedented preparation and planning in exchange for a wealth of understanding about space and basic survival.

"We experienced a 45% reduction in R&D budgets during the process of getting Constellation up and running," said Dr. Jeff Davis, Director of the Space Life Sciences Directorate (SLSD) at NASA's Johnson Space Center in Houston. "We knew those resources weren't coming back and we thought to ourselves, we can't get this done by just doing 45% less, we need to approach this whole program in a new way."

Realizing it must redefine its program within resource constraints, Jeff and his team (some 160 civil servants and 800 contractors) opened their minds to new ways of imagining work, resourcing, and even innovation itself.

"Early the next year, in 2006, we ran a visioning exercise that outlined four possible future scenarios," he said. "We selected the one that focused on forming alliances to leverage our internal work. We then wrote a strategic plan in 2007 and conducted a benchmark study focused on forming alliances. In our study, we found that alliance forming organizations routinely scored high in measures of their ability to produce innovations."

Later, after Davis and his team took a course at Harvard Business School titled "Leading Change and Organization Renewal" (LCOR), the SLSD began its pursuit of open innovation in earnest. To begin, the SLSD reviewed the gaps in its research and development portfolio and ran a portfolio mapping exercise designed by Prof. Gary Pisano at Harvard Business School on "the four ways to collaborate."

Davis said, "We had pretty complete coverage in the quadrant labeled 'hierarchical and closed'—but we quickly learned that if we wanted to close the gaps in our total innovation program, we needed to better leverage external innovation platforms."

"It was," he said, "a thorough process of defining our entire body of work, evaluating which pieces we wanted to keep inside versus outside, defining gaps, and finally assessing which innovation model made sense for each gap area. But you have to take it *that* seriously, and do the homework or you'll miss opportunities. This has been a four-year journey for us. Then, in 2010, the Office of Management and Budget published guidance on using prizes to stimulate innovation, and we realized our efforts were aligned with an overall strategy of the Federal government."

Davis and his team had become aware of InnoCentive through the Harvard course and shortly thereafter NASA began a pilot program with InnoCentive (one of three overall that included Yet2.com and TopCoder), the Waltham-based innovation marketplace, to run seven "high-value challenges" that NASA felt would benefit from the "innovation mall" model of open collaboration.

Participants from around the world, 579 of them, took a close look at the "Data-Driven Forecasting of Solar Events" challenge on InnoCentive's website. The problem was finding a suitable method to more reliably predict the particle storms originating with solar events. These storm's particles can be a hazard to spacecraft and astronauts above the earth's atmosphere. They also impact weather. Fourteen complete proposed solutions were submitted. After reviewing them, NASA issued a success award to Bruce Cragin, a semiretired radio frequency engineer.

Cragin holds a bachelor of science degree in engineering physics and a doctorate in applied physics. He has 15 years experience in plasma physics basic research and another 13 years of industrial experience as a radio frequency engineer.

The challenge was "right in the 'sweet-spot,'" Cragin said, "Though I hadn't worked in the area of solar physics as such, I had thought a lot about the theory of magnetic reconnection. Also, the image analysis skills I acquired in the 1980s, while looking into some-thing called the 'small comet hypothesis,' turned out to be very useful." As with many novel ideas, the fusion of skills and specific experiences enabled Cragin to see the problem and propose a solution that had escaped others focused primarily on the discipline of solar physics.

And as Cragin "daisy-chains" these cross-disciplinary approaches, he notes that the work he did on the NASA challenge, "focused my attention on predictive modeling. That led to another challenge involving maize genetics to which I also submitted a solution, and became a finalist. The computational tools acquired in that work are now being applied in two additional challenges, both genetics-related."

"The NASA employees who write, run, and evaluate our chal-lenges are converts and advocates of open innovation because they get good results," said Dr. Jennifer Fogarty, Space Life Sciences Innovation Lead.

Davis, who is leading this transformation, didn't always find the going easy. Many of those who prospered under an old framework of innovation emerged initially as skeptics. For example, some won-dered how can you solve a major solar physics problem without years of steeping in solar physics research and study? However, the fruits of this effort are becoming increasingly apparent to his organization and to NASA as a whole. Leaders such as Davis are mapping the frontiers of innovation as they map the frontiers of space. Davis said: "Other disciplines in NASA are now considering conducting challenges based on our experience. Our experiences with open innovation have created an opportunity for us to be thought leaders in this practice; our early experiences show that open innovation is faster and more cost-effective than some traditional problem-solving tools. We're now working on a decision framework to determine how newer and older problem-solving methods work best together. And, there's a real ele-ment of fun and participation to it. It changes how you think."

# 4

# The Long Tail of Expertise

"We sold more books today that didn't sell at all yesterday than we sold today of all the books that did sell yesterday."
—*Josh Petersen, Amazon employee*[1]

## Overview

Whoever thought the power function would become an icon of popular culture? Chris Anderson's and Clay Shirky's terrific writings have achieved just that. The power function, once relegated to workhorse status in statistics, mathematics, and modeling, now graces the cover of popular books and appears in hip, trendy magazines. Its newfound status results in the ease in which it explains the market phenomenon of businesses such as Amazon.com.

The Long Tail concept has found applications in marketing, inventory strategy, Internet statistics, research, and media sales. It is invoked here, qualitatively, as a means to illustrate some observations made on a daily basis at InnoCentive and which are more broadly applicable to innovation in general and the entire notion of expertise. Step one is for you to have a clear picture of the image in mind as the arguments are discussed. A power function plot, with its long tail is shown in Figure 4.1.

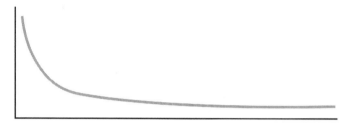

**Figure 4.1   A plot of a power function showing the very long tail that approaches, but never quite reaches, the baseline as it extends forever to the right.**

For the moment, concentrate only on the curved gray line that swoops down from the upper left and disappears off the chart on the lower right. The right portion of this curve is what has been referred to as **the long tail**. For this discussion, the left side will be called **the head**, in contrast to **the tail**. Using the bookselling example, you can label the y-axis **sales volume** (or popularity, if you prefer). And the x-axis would be simply each book in the world arrayed from most popular at present on the left to least popular on the right. The head of this curve would thus contain those books on *The New York Times* bestseller list, and anything mentioned on the Oprah Winfrey show. If you are a small bookseller and have room for only 100 titles, naturally you would want the 100 books represented on the leftmost part of this curve—for the simple reason that they would generate more revenue per inch of shelf space than any other 100 books. The point made by Anderson and the long tail argument is this: On any given day, customers are more likely to want to purchase more books from the hundred-and first-popularity on *down* than they are books among the 100 most popular. But because you don't know precisely which of those less popular books are likely to be purchased that day, you can never make a rational stocking decision other than the one already made, which is to stock the most popular books.

These arguments are, at the same time, obvious and subtle. Businesses make such rational choices all the time, and because of their obviousness, their subtlety is never examined.

# Defining and Hiring Experts

Expanding on the ideas briefly introduced in Chapter 3, "A New Innovation Framework," the way in which this long tail argument creeps into hiring practices—and even the notions by which expertise and qualifications are defined—will be discussed. This will be followed by an examination of the subtle consequences of continuing to practice in that way.

Most people feel that they are quite clear on their definition of what qualifies someone to be called an expert. It is easy for them to say that Stephen Hawking is an expert in cosmology and I am not, that Jared is an expert woodworker and I am not, that I am an expert chemist and Dwayne is not, and that Dwayne is an expert mathematician and I am not. Such statements feel well-defined and easily justifiable on the basis of degrees, training, experience, publications, and contributions. But, even as I exclude myself from the category of expert plumbers, I would argue that, although I know less than those experts, I *do* know more than many other people. And there are those who know more than me but may not quite reach the level of "expert."

Recognizing the continuous nature of these definitions, you can realize that no boundary line exists and that experts merge seamlessly with novices and even those who can be described only as totally ignorant on the subject of plumbing.

The first reaction to an argument like this is understandably, "So what?" So what if it's a continuum; so what if you have to draw some arbitrary line? So what if you make the measured decision to use your neighbor's Saturday plumbing skills to put in a new sink instead of hiring an enormously qualified, and probably overpaid, expert? Baseball pitching skills probably follow the same continuous pattern, and the Yankees are content to look for the pitcher residing on the leftmost of the curve and offer him a sufficient salary to entice him to join the team.

All hiring decisions are generally presented as if it were no more complex than the recruiting of a new pitcher or making that Saturday afternoon plumbing choice. But in the case of full-time permanent employment offers, it is often quite a bit murkier. One typically frames the recruiting process in those same simple terms: "Find me a top-grade CEO," "Find me an expert electrical engineer," or "Find me an outstanding market analyst." But the commitment of hiring a permanent employee is actually quite different. You might even have an immediate situation driving your choice. Perhaps a new CEO is needed to help enter a new market sector or to manage through an explosive period of growth. Perhaps an electrical engineer is needed to debug stray radio frequency signals that are compromising a new product release. And perhaps a market analyst is needed to immediately prepare reports on newly acquired telecom capabilities. But it is almost invariably true that if these individuals are hired, they will remain with the organization after, sometimes long after, those immediate needs are satisfied.

Executives, human resource departments, and recruiters are smart enough to recognize that they are seeking a broader sort of individual, one who can solve not only the issues of immediate concern but also the issues, appropriate to their expertise, that will surface in the future. Unfortunately, because these are issues and challenges that *haven't* surfaced yet, they cannot be named, and they cannot be specifically recruited for. And thus, the practical consequence of "expertise" within the business world becomes awkwardly defined as "the ability to solve a domain-specific problem posed in the future." It's not a real crisp definition; it's not a definition you would look forward to building metrics around. It's just the practical reality of what you're actually doing when you hire someone.

You hire an editor because you believe she will do a good job of editing manuscripts that haven't been written yet; you hire a chemist because you believe she will do a good job of synthesizing compounds, that not only do not exist yet, but also which, at present, you do not even know you want; and you hire a bookkeeper to compute unmade sales, unmade costs, and use reporting rules yet unwritten by accounting standards bodies.

So how, exactly, can you measure a job candidate's fitness for a *future* need? The answer to this question is why this entire book began with a quote about gambling and horse racing: "The race is not always to the swift, nor the battle to the strong, but that's the way to bet." Employers are placing bets on employees, and their recruitment filters are designed to identify "the swift and the strong." Is that not what a race handicapping system is designed to do? It is designed to use measurements that can be made today to enable you to predict the horse and jockey that will win tomorrow. The values that can be measured today, such as recent track times, health, weight, experience, and so on, are not the values crucial to your success; that is, all you really want to know at the moment it counts is, "Did the horse win?" Those other properties you measure aren't what you actually *want* to know; they are simply what you *can* know, and their use is predicated on a belief that they are related, in some predictable fashion, to what it is you actually want to know. This is how races are handicapped; this is how employment is handicapped, this is how expertise is handicapped. The measures may be different, but the principles are the same.

It's time to take another look at the long tail and its head of expertise. Figure 4.2 fills in this newly articulated definition of the y-axis, relevant to the employment process. There are also zone labels and shading on this graph to enable you to more conveniently track the arguments that follow. You recognize the ultimate unmeasurability of this Y-value, but engage in a little thought experiment and pretend that such a measurement is possible for the sake of the following.

Via the collation of degrees, prior jobs, recommendations, grades, and so on, you can assume that you have hired well. You have recruited employees that lie to the leftmost of the chart. You have

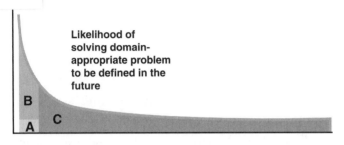

Figure 4.2   Three zones of the long tail curve. Zones A and B are our defined "experts." It is them we seek to employ to bring us innovations. But we always employ a minority as in Zone A, while the majority of experts work elsewhere, Zone B. Generally ignored is the zone of greatest overall area (cumulative probability in this graph), Zone C. See text for tapping this enormous resource for innovation.

stocked your limited bookshelves with *The New York Times* bestsellers and the book recommendations of Oprah Winfrey. But now say it again. You have stocked your limited bookshelves with *only The New York Times* bestsellers and the book recommendations of Oprah Winfrey. Of course you have only stocked *some* of each of these key assets. As already pointed out—most of the smart people don't work for you. You have hired those shown in Zone A in Figure 4.2. The skilled employees your competitors have collectively hired are those shown in the larger Zone B.

# The Untapped Potential

Executives listen to Bill Joy and worry about the relative size of Zone B; he's right—most of the smart people work for somebody else. And you can worry that your employees are being wooed by those competitors, even as you woo the employees of your competitors. All the while, Zone C, the long tail, remains out of your thoughts. And why shouldn't it remain unthought-of? There's only so much shelf space. Why waste it? This is what Chris Anderson describes as the logic of scarcity. A logic that seems less and less applicable to the Internet age.

The logic of plenty says, "Look at Zone C!" It's not just bigger than Zone A; it's bigger than Zones A and B combined. The, at first dubious, and certainly nonobvious, conclusion is that there is more problem-solving capability among the "less qualified" than there is in the "more qualified" populations. How can that be? Simple. There are *more* people less qualified—many more people less qualified— many, many, many more people less qualified. The long tail of skills has always been—and is today—largely untapped and institutionally discounted. The tapping of this long tail, Zone C, in spite of the technical correctness of the arguments just made, still feels wrong; it still feels like a bad idea.

Why would you hire a computer hobbyist or a construction engineer, when you need the best electrical engineer possible? Of course you would not. It is the history of "innovating from within," of cloaking your innovation processes in secrecy, that compels you to too readily equate commercial innovation with hiring innovators. Tapping into the enormous capacity of the long tail *cannot* be done via the hiring process—and therefore cannot be part of closed innovation. It's not that history isn't full of stories of problems solved by innovations coming from the tail, of breakthroughs put forward by the tail. Some have been mentioned and will be mentioned again: patent clerks rewriting cosmology, telecom engineers predicting solar particle storms, weekend handymen contributing to environmental cleanup, and patent attorneys designing new routes to poly-carboxylic acids. But wait! Some of these examples are probably not a familiar part of your college coursework. That's okay, they're everyday experiences for those who help the world tap into this long tail of knowledge and expertise—and replace the logic of innovation scarcity with the logic of innovation plenty. And you'll find each of those stories in this book.

Perhaps one of the earliest, and most systematic, attempts to document the contributions of a portion of Zone C to product innovation is the effort of Eric von Hippel at MIT's Sloan School of Business. Von Hippel is the author of *Democratizing Innovation* (referenced earlier). Using a long tail argument of his own, von Hippel defines an easily identifiable cohort of "nonexperts," which in our imagery would be the occupants of the left side of Zone C—the head of the tail as it were. In other words, if you were to undertake the tapping of Zone C for ideas, von Hippel defines a protocol for rapidly identifying the potentially most productive members of that zone. von Hippel calls these key contributors "lead users." They may lack engineering and design qualifications that product companies seek in their R&D staff, but they are the customers who buy the company's products. Actually they are a special subset of customers; they are the ones who fearlessly dismantle them and tweak them for purposes of their own. They are the gearheads of the 1950s unbolting the stock carburetor from their newly purchased Mercury and ultimately extracting another 10hp from the engine. Because they are the buyers, and they can often be identified, they represent a readily tapped portion of Zone C that it is inexcusable for business to leave unexploited.

# Tackling the Long Tail

Power functions have an interesting property known as **self simi-larity**, which is to say that if you take any part of the function, it still looks like the whole function. So as you peer into Zone C—and exclude for a moment Zones A and B—the lead users become the "experts" in the "head" of Zone C, and the *remainder* of Zone C becomes—yet again—the zone of greater cumulative opportunity—another long tail!

Although historical attempts have been made to tap the tail, and are recorded elsewhere in this text—for example, the Orteig Prize (for crossing the Atlantic), the Longitude Prize, and the Millennium Prizes in mathematics—the Internet has opened Zone C possibilities hitherto unimagined. Platforms have emerged that enable challenges and needs to be broadcast and potential solutions to be acquired from *all three* zones, with indifference to source.

In early academic analyses of such systems, this approach was dubbed "broadcast search" by Harvard Business School professor Karim Lahkani and his co-authors.[2] They have identified several Internet platforms, such as Topcoder and InnoCentive, and at least semi-quantitatively confirmed the Zone shadings in Figure 4.2, which is to say that a great many of the crowd-sourced successful solutions are originating from sources that would not have been placed, *a priori*, in the leftmost portion of the curve. As stated in one paper by Lakhani, along with Lars Jeppeson, Peter Lohse, and Jill Panetta, "Problem-solving success was found to be associated with the ability to attract specialized solvers with a range of diverse scientific interests. Furthermore, successful solvers solved problems at the boundary or outside of their fields of expertise, indicating a transfer of knowledge from one field to others."[3]

It would be nice to have a direct "head to tail" comparison of the problem-solving effectiveness of the different zones. And several exist in today's business literature. One such example appeared in the NASA case at the end of the previous chapter. A solution that had been sought for about 30 years within Zone A was solved in months when Zone C was tapped.

Perhaps the best, prospectively designed study was carried out under the direction of Tod Bedilion, director of technology management of Roche Diagnostics. Roche took a problem that had been worked on over many years by both Roche and its partners. The challenge was to quantify a flowing clinical sample. The challenge was then broadcast to researchers globally throughout Roche and after collecting proposed solutions, the challenge was then posted to the large InnoCentive network of diverse solvers. At the time of posting, InnoCentive was unaware that this challenge had the history just described. Over the posting period, the challenge was viewed by almost 1000 solvers and 113 proposals were submitted from all around the world. In an article by London Business School professor Julian Birkinshaw and the editor of *Business Strategy Review*, Stuart

Crainer, Bedilion is quoted: "The proposals were incredible... In contrast to the internal network, rather than being one or two lines, many were multiple pages. Some people had done experiments. There were diagrams. There were drawings that filled an entire notebook. We would have been delighted if we could have got much of the work out of our own research organization... I couldn't put ten people in a room and have a brainstorming session or a seminar for two days for the same cost with all the travel involved. And I would have gotten a few hundred sticky notes rather than an entire notebook with 113 separate detailed proposals." The authors go on to say, "And, most important of all, there was a result. Basically, in 60 days, Roche was able to solve a problem that it and its partner have been tinkering with and optimizing for the last 15 years."[4]

Reinforcing the non-cash utility arguments put forth in Chapter 2, "The Future of Value Creation," Bedilion observes, "Clearly, the financial incentive played a part here, but we think there is more going on—people also seem to get intrinsic value out of sharing their expertise through this community." Bedilion's observation mirrors that made years earlier by Lakhani as he examined the motivations of InnoCentive solvers. In the same Lakhani paper cited earlier, it is noted that the likelihood of making a winning submission correlates more strongly with intrinsic motivations, such as the satisfaction of problem-solving or intellectual curiosity, than it does with the cash award (though not statistically different).[5] This is, of course, not an argument to abandon cash bounties, but a recognition that multiple utilities are in play and important to the process. Many authors have commented on the "wisdom of crowds," putatively starting with James Surowiecki's book by the same name.[6] Enormous efforts are made to define and measure collective intelligence, including multidisciplinary undertakings such as the MIT Center for Collective Intelligence, under the direction of Professor Thomas Malone. Following are a few of the authors' own observations about where the problem-solving value of Zone C, taken as a whole, originates. Out of respect for the scholarly work in the categorizing and measuring of crowd intelligence, you are referred to elsewhere for in-depth scientific arguments. But we do not shy away from addressing the question of just where the solving power comes from in a crowd. It would be too simple to just shrug and imagine that broadcasting challenges to the crowd precipitates out the occasional expert or near-expert: the needle-in-a-haystack argument. And that happens; but that is about finding needles, a search problem, and not the power of the crowd as a whole, as a body. Legitimately, it would seem that the only explanation needed is the "long-ness" of the tail and the summing of many small probabilities versus the summing of a few larger ones. But our own observations of problems, solved in a broadcast search or crowd-sourced manner, prompt us to propose three characteristics of the crowd—three origins of its problem-solving capability: **diversity**, **marginality**, and **serendipity**.

# Diversity, Marginality, and Serendipity

The first of these is **diversity**. Having a larger number of people tackle a problem would obviously be of limited use if they all used the same approach. This is more than just a numbers game as in "many hands make light work." A mental picture of the diversity argument is to imagine "space." Although this actual space is "problem-solving space," with the axes defined by the parameters of the approach, imagining that space familiar to all of us, as a great celestial vacuum, sparsely populated by stars, will work perfectly well for this metaphor. One characteristic of rich, complex problems is that there are so many ways NOT to solve them.

Think of the few scattered stars in a volume of space as being solutions to your problem and the cold dark areas representing failure to solve the problem. Problem solving routinely begins with a hypothesis or a belief of what a solution *might* be. If that first attempt fails, the results of the effort are gathered and analyzed, and a new attempt is made. Think of that problem-solving process as an explorer. The testing of an hypothesis is the equivalent of that explorer stepping into space where he thinks there is a star, a solution to his problem. His analyses, calculations, and logic have led him to *guess* where a star might be, and he steps into space to find his surroundings cold and inhospitable with only a glimmer of light in the distance. He takes stock of the situation and jumps again, pausing to assess his new location. He does this repeatedly, each time his evaluations telling him if he is "getting warmer." And thus he navigates his way from his original guess to the solution-star.

Now, imagine instead that you have not one explorer but a thousand explorers. Each of these explorers begins with a different perspective on where a star might be found. They each begin with different instruments to do the calculations. They each begin with different experiences and intuitions about finding stars. And so they each jump into a different region of space. These are not random jumps. If they were, then, in all likelihood, every one of our thousand explorers would find themselves cold and dark. They are informed jumps (though to varying degrees) and as such it is not unimaginable that some would find themselves in regions relatively warm and bright with only a short distance remaining to a solution.

## A Thousand and One Explorers or How to Find a Star

In the sciences, we often use space and dimensions to characterize a system. It isn't a space of directions, but a space of properties. Sometimes it is called phase space, which helps make it clear that it isn't "good old-fashioned space" we're talking about. (But in some disciplines that too has a specific meaning.) The metaphor may not be familiar to lots of people, but the concept is easy to grasp.

If we use the challenge of "invent an electric light bulb," we might create problem-solving space as follows: We can have one axis of "space" that is a composition of the filament, as opposed to say, east-west. And we can have another dimension that is not north-south, but composition of the atmosphere inside the bulb, and we can have a third dimension that is not up-down, but is voltage applied to the filament. (There are dozens of additional axes or parameters of light bulb design, but we'll ignore all but three for this example.) In regular space, we might speak of something to be found 5 miles north, 2 miles west, and at an altitude of 2000 ft. In our light-bulb space, we might choose to conduct an experiment at the point in space characterized by filament = carbon, atmosphere = oxygen, and voltage = 1,000. Of course, we get just a brief bright flash. It is a failure as a light bulb.

Most points in space (distinct combinations of filament material, bulb filler, and voltage) give failures, just like real space is mostly emptiness. A few give actual light bulbs. Filament = tungsten, atmosphere = vacuum, and voltage = 120 is just one of those combinations; that is the familiar bulb you have in your table lamp. In this simple example, there are literally millions or billions of possibilities. Most fail. A few succeed. Searching them is the metaphoric equivalent of searching real space looking for stars.

Classic innovation is to enter space and begin "tacking" toward a star. Slow. Laborious. Filled with failure. Thomas Edison famously said, "I now know 10,000 ways NOT to make a light bulb." (And funders paid for *every* failure.)

The InnoCentive approach is to commission ten thousand and one explorers. They all enter space at different points: 10,000 fail. One lands on a star. He or she gets paid. The 10,000 that fail go their way. They don't get paid. But in the process they have mapped, in months, a region of "space" that could take decades to explore in a serial, step-wise fashion. And, because there isn't just one star (solution), but many, they may likely have found the unexpected solution that changes the game for future explorations. At the heart, it is a business model founded on parallel problem-solving and paying for solutions, not efforts.

**Marginality** is the second source of problem-solving capability in the crowd. Although you have become acclimated to the notion that deference to experts is a wise choice of action, you need to recognize that the acquisition of expertise is inevitably accompanied by the acquisition of constraints. Experts are taught not only to solve problems but also *how* to solve them. They are taught that there are right approaches and wrong approaches. They are taught what has been tried and failed, and should not be tried again. These constraints may hinder their ability to see problems in a fresh light and approach them without bias. We are not suggesting that experts are miseducated or maltrained; recall from the arguments about the long tail that the experts resided at the highest probability, the "head" of the graph, and *that* by virtue of their education and training. And if, contrary to the counsel of Runyon, the race was *always* to the swift and the strong, you would need to proceed no further. But because you know this not to be the case, you need to accept that constraints go hand-in-hand with expertise. This has led to attempts to measure those biases and deal with them explicitly. In a publication draft that Karim Lakhani shared with us, he wrote: "Because individuals become socialized to the norms and beliefs of their fields and organizations, remaining at the margins while keeping up to date and actively pursuing access to resources offers those marginalized a different set of perspectives and heuristics than those at the core of the professional establishment."[7] Such observations have been published, in connection with broadcast search methodology, in a Lakhani and Jeppeson article in Organizational Science,[8] and in the arena of psychology and sociology, in Neil McLaughlin's article in Sociological Quarterly, appropriately titled *"Optimal Marginality."*[9]

Our third and final argument for the source of problem-solving capability within a crowd is **serendipity**. The role of serendipity is not an unfamiliar one, and it is discussed at the conclusion this chapter with a retelling of the story of Archimedes, in an attempt to extract new learning's from an old tale. Serendipity seems for the most part to be one of those factors completely outside the control of either the institution or the individual attempting to invent or innovate. And yet, its importance to the advancement of knowledge and technology is evident in the lore—whether you speak of Newton getting beaned by an Apple, Kekule dreaming of snakes, Maxwell's envisioning of gear trains, or Archimede's "Eureka!" bath.

These historical observations, along with your own personal experiences in solving complex problems should lead you to conclude that novel solutions often arise due to the confluence of three distinct factors: skill or training, a clearly articulated challenge or need, and a personal experience (not domain experience), either past or present (usually viewed as the *source* of the serendipity).

# The Tear Gas Connection

Our experience at InnoCentive, where we have watched the crowd solve problems hundreds of times over, leads us to repeated observations about how, and how frequently, these three factors of diversity, marginality, and serendipity, play a role in bringing forward novel problem-solving approaches. Although we could illustrate this with a great number of examples, let's choose just one to show how *all* three forces were at work.

An InnoCentive client had an application for a tetracarboxylic acid, a novel molecule, that was not readily produced at a competitive cost. The challenge to design an efficient means of preparing this material was posted on the InnoCentive website and attracted potential solvers from around the world. During the 4 months that the challenge was active, 247 people from 35 countries, representing 247 jumps into problem-solving space (diversity)—opened project rooms to see the details of the challenge and sign intellectual property transfer agreements. At the conclusion of the 125-day posting period, 17 individuals had submitted novel proposed solutions. In a blinded review of these submissions, by the seeker, the most promising approach was submitted by a patent attorney. To be fair, the attorney, David Bradin, was no stranger to chemistry and had worked as a chemist before earning his law degree: marginality.

You might ask, "Where's the serendipity?" After being announced as the winning solver, Bradin explained that when he first saw the problem his thoughts turned immediately to tear gas and some chemical strategies used in its preparation. In an obtuse series of mental links, Bradin applied his tear gas experiences to seeing the problem in a new way.

Of course, that's not to say that "tear gas" was the only potential provocation or experience that would enable a fresh perspective. But in as much as it is virtually impossible to apply serendipitous connections or events to rational problem solving, it seems that the only logical resort is to a crowd—opening up a greater likelihood of such connections occurring. Bradin says that he continues to scan the challenges posted as part of the InnoCentive website, "for those where I might have a flash of insight." This is clearly a matching mechanism that is not operating when challenging research problems are assigned within an institution.

# Eureka! The Right Question at the Right Time

As briefly mentioned, in connection with serendipity, the role of the challenge is not to be ignored in capitalizing on the intelligent behavior of the system. This can be illustrated by recalling the oft *untold* portions of the Archimedes story and the discovery of buoyancy or water displacement. Hiero, the tyrant of Syracuse, had ordered an artisan to construct a crown for him. The tyrant had paid for the crown and supplied all the gold that was to be used. Naturally Hiero was smart enough to have the crown weighed upon its receipt to ensure that all the gold was accounted for. But amalgams and alloys were known to the people of Hiero's time. Gold was strengthened by the addition of base metals without significantly altering its appearance. How was Hiero to know that the gold he delivered had not had a portion removed and the remainder mixed with lead to produce the expected weight. Well, one feature of the alloy, gold plus lead, was that it would have a different density; that is, the weight of a given volume of the alleged gold mixture would not be the same as that of pure gold. Hiero could verify the honesty of the artisan by measuring the volume of the crown.

For this, he took it a local citizen skilled in the art of mathematics. Archimedes examined the crown, acknowledged the beautiful workmanship, and then delivered the bad news: The crown was an irregularly shaped object, and although Archimedes could easily have delivered to Hiero the accurate volume of a cube or a sphere, or even a cylinder, he could not do so for an irregularly shaped crown. And, of course, melting the crown back into a cube would've merely started the process all over again (although possibly with a new, live artisan).

That night, as the tale is usually told, Archimedes retired to his home and took a bath. As he lowered himself into the tub, he noticed the water rising along the sides of his "regularly shaped" bath receptacle. As Archimedes watched, he realized this was a method to effectively measure the volume of an irregularly shaped object, whether that irregularly shaped object was Archimedes' middle-aged body or Hiero's ornate crown. As the story goes, Archimedes was so excited that he leapt from the tub, never bothering to dress, and ran naked through the streets of Syracuse shouting, "Eureka! Eureka. I have found it. I have found it."

This story is related to high school science classes as an illustration of creativity, the "a-ha! moment." Students are encouraged to remain inquisitive about their world, to realize that clever solutions to problems may very well lie outside the present day strictures of what is known, and that even complex mathematical problems may have a simple nonmathematical solution. Less attention is paid to Hiero's role in this process other than as a setup for the important event that was to follow. (Chapter 6, "The Challenge Driven Enterprise," discusses the topic of the challenge's role as well.)

But let's here illustrate the criticality of Hiero's question, and the manner in which it was posed, by speculating (probably rightly) on something not recorded in either history nor this oft-told anecdote. This wasn't Archimedes first bath!

How was it that this math- and science-oriented, intelligent person had failed to discover a breakthrough—that sent him screaming naked through the streets—on any of his many prior baths? We are prone to think of questions and challenges as necessary precedents to discovery, without delving much more deeply into how they are constructed, what properties make them powerful, or even where they came from in the first place. Everyone is familiar with clever courtroom dramas in which the nuanced wording of the question either elicits an incriminating response, or in which the question itself contains a conclusion that the attorney wants the jury to hear. Advances in science and technology are rarely considered in light of that courtroom drama. They are not considered exercises in wordplay. You can imagine that they live in a realm somewhere above language—independent, a consequence of laws that exist free of what they are named or even how they are described.

But scientific and technological advance do not occur at a constant rate and on all fronts simultaneously. They are sparked by something. The frontiers are moving in fits and starts according to human conditions, human desires, and human language. The salient difference between Archimedes' 10,001st bath and his 10,000th was Hiero's question, and, no doubt, Hiero's enormous control over the consequences of the answer. It is a given that, almost certainly, this principle would have been discovered either at another time or in another place.

Hiero's query acted as what Professor Paul Carlile, at Boston University's School School of Management, calls a **boundary object**, which is a device, either conceptual or physical, that enables a boundary of some type to be crossed.[10] These could be boundaries of academic disciplines, boundaries of terrain—that is, water and land—or boundaries of time. The circumstances of Hiero's question produced a shift in time and space so that an event occurred at this particular point in time and space rather than at some other. Challenges, or well-formulated questions-asked, are the boundary objects that enable human progress to occur as it does, in fits and starts, and the effectiveness of that progress is often a function of the effectiveness of the challenge itself. As frequently remarked, "A problem well-stated is a problem half solved."

The tale of Archimedes is told here not only for its obvious messages regarding creativity and innovation, but also to suggest that it could be practiced by innovators in a much more plentiful, more accessible, manner. It is common experience that serendipity is shrugged off as one of those things that just sometimes happens when your head is down and you're working hard. It's good, but it's not schedulable; it can't be invoked at will—but is also not an entirely rare occurrence. To access it, and to do so consciously, means a crowd is indispensable. When looking for a unique solution, the key, with foresight, would be not just to ask an Archimedes, but to ask him as he lowers himself into his bath. Unfortunately, we don't have foresight. To mimic that result, you need to access many potential sources of knowledge, each engaging in a unique train of thought. You need to find Bradin as he thinks of tear gas, and all you know for sure is that he occupies a crowd, a crowd that must become part of your overall problem-solving strategy—a crowd accessible only if your organization taps Zone C, the long tail. Goodbye to the logic of scarcity; welcome to the logic of plenty.

As Anderson himself explains in his October 2004 *Wired* article, "What's really amazing about the Long Tail is the sheer size of it. Combine enough nonhits on the Long Tail and you've got a market bigger than the hits. Take books: The average Barnes & Noble carries

130,000 titles. Yet more than half of Amazon's book sales come from *outside* its top 130,000 titles. Consider the implication: If the Amazon statistics are any guide, the market for books that are not even sold in the average bookstore is larger than the market for those that are."[11]

The history of innovation is marked by many events in which the uniquely prepared mind capitalized on a singular set of circumstances. In the last century, centers have been built for innovation and technical excellence by application of the rules of rational compromise and the logic of scarcity. Admittedly, you still can't program serendipity into the process, *per se*, but you can employ the crowd and the logic of abundance to create a greater likelihood of serendipity and other problem-solving opportunities to be manifest. Rephrasing Anderson's comment on "non-hits," and speaking of any specific well-stated challenge, you might say, "The number of novel ideas available from those who aren't 'experts' is greater than the number of novel ideas available from those who are." This open approach to problem solving can open the door to accelerated innovation and to solutions to globally critical problems of nourishment, environment, health, and energy. Can you really afford to leave any zone in your map of human capability untapped?

# Case Study: How the Oil Spill Recovery Institute Tapped the Crowd to Be Better Prepared for Arctic Spills[12]

On March 24, 1989, the massive oil tanker, Exxon Valdez, hit Bligh Reef and ruptured, spilling 11 million gallons of crude oil into Alaska's Prince William Sound. The Exxon Valdez disaster affected 1,300 miles of coastline and threatened many species of wildlife from fish to mammals to birds and even insects and bacteria.

The Exxon Valdez case has been studied by numerous researchers and is taught in colleges and universities around the world. The facts of this event live on in secondary school textbooks on science and the environment. While Prince William Sound recovers, and even as oil remains on some of the beaches, 20 years later, it is vitally important that plans are made NOW to obviate, or at least mediate, any future spills and the environmental consequences.

The Oil Pollution Act, passed by Congress in 1990 in response to the Valdez disaster, created the Oil Spill Recovery Institute, headquartered in the Prince William Sound Science Center in Cordova, Alaska. Subsequent legislation has insured that the Institute and its mandate will persist as long as drilling efforts continue in Alaska.

As they have for two decades, OSRI continues to play out scenarios and evaluate potential responses. At a conference several years ago, it brainstormed some of the unique hurdles it may face in a future arctic spill and agreed to collect, study, and document the potential responses. One clear complication of an arctic spill is the frigid temperature. Among the tools available during cleanup is the skimmer vessel known as a minibarge. These hold about 250 barrels (a little over 10,000 gallons) of crude oil, mixed with seawater, as the surface water is skimmed and deposited into the tanks. When the tank on a minibarge is full, the contents must be moved to a larger vessel or to holding tanks along the shoreline.

If it's –10 degrees Fahrenheit (and it often is), the oil is going to thicken beyond the point of transferability. The pumps used to transfer the oil are powerful submersion pumps that are designed to be dropped directly into the minibarge holding tanks. Although capable of transferring something as viscous as peanut butter, it is imagined that in a frozen minibarge tank, the running pump would simply "chew" its way to the bottom, leaving a slowly collapsing hole and emptying the tank only over a prohibitively long time. If a method could be found for expeditiously emptying the barges in the coldest weather, it would speed cleanup and provide reserve barge capacity year-round as a safeguard.

OSRI is a grant-making body, funding research related to oil spill recovery at high latitudes. Lead by research program director Scott

Pegau, it identifies and funds research to address gaps in understanding and capabilities. As Pegau says, "This specific problem (of cold, viscous oil transfer) has been around for years—as have many others." Over time, Pegau and his team have consulted with petroleum engineers from around the world. Wanting to explore beyond the real-world constraints he had to work with, Pegau turned to a problem-solving network, InnoCentive. The challenge for "reducing viscous shear" was posted on InnoCentive and broadcast to solvers in 120 nations. At the end of the posting period, there were 27 submitted responses to the challenge. Of these, four different ideas were deemed worthy of further consideration, and one was awarded the bounty OSRI had posted. Pegau recognized that many promising leads were coming from those who had never worked with oil but who recognized the similarities in behavior to other materials with which they did have experience.

The winning approach came from an industrial hygienist who spent his typical day measuring workplace exposure to hazardous materials. John Davis, the awarded solver, has a master's degree in chemistry from Illinois State University. Under the direction of Professor Cheryl Stevenson, his thesis project was "Anion Radicals of Cyclooctatetraene." There was virtually no connection between his professional specialties and the OSRI needs. But Davis sees himself, first and foremost, as a problem solver, and he could readily grasp the nature of OSRI's problem. In past efforts, Davis was helping a friend and found himself pouring concrete. It was while on the construction site that Davis learned how to manage the movement of highly viscous fluids, such as setting concrete. As a scientist, it was readily apparent to him that the techniques he'd employed pouring cement could be an answer to moving the oil off those frozen barges.

Davis' solution involved the use of sonic vibrations to "mobilize" the fluid and cause it to behave as if it were a much less-viscous substance. Using methods proven elsewhere, he postulated that the sonically agitated oil would "vibrate" its way into the pumps under the available pressures and allow itself to be pumped away from the barges so that they could return to their duty of skimming the spill. So, what Davis proposed, in a nutshell, was the use of sounds to save our sounds. Luckily, there have been no new spills in Alaska, but if and when there are, this new technique is now "in the quiver" to respond rapidly and minimize their impact.

Even before Scott Pegau's arrival at OSRI, the Institute had considered using public challenges and awards to advance its research agenda and solve some of the unique problems it faced. But no clear mechanism had been identified until the InnoCentive platform was launched and provided a low-cost access to promotion, challenge structuring, and a widely accessed web presence. Working with InnoCentive, OSRI had placed a "bounty" on solving this problem of $20,000.

Since their success with this first challenge, OSRI has posted five additional challenges on InnoCentive. Collectively, the challenges produced 215 submitted ideas, and OSRI has made awards on three of the five. It is a source of hope that OSRI and clever solvers are openly collaborating to ensure that future adverse environmental impacts are minimized.

# 5

## The Selection of Appropriate Innovation Channels

> "I dreamed a thousand new paths.... I woke and walked my old one."
>
> —*Chinese proverb*

## Overview

Consider the opening quote in this chapter less one of guidance and more of a cautionary tale. Leaders, as noted in much greater detail in Chapter 9, "Leadership," bring to reality that which they dream. And though there may not be a thousand paths discussed below, of the multiple paths available, too few are trod in most organizations at present.

This chapter is going to switch gears. Up until now, we've spoken about the changes that open innovation brings and argued its merits as a means of diversifying problem solving approaches, reducing false negatives, sharing and managing risk and thereby improving the overall productivity of your innovation engine, whether those innovations are for delineating new marketing campaigns, improving business strategy, or designing future products and services. But even solid portfolio arguments don't always help those where the rubber hits the road. Many project workers and department supervisors see only the

project. In fact, they often have no accountability for the overall performance of the portfolio but are keenly accountable for how well a
given project is executed. They need to often make channel choices
based on what's best for the project or a portion of the project and so
this chapter has been constrained to those arguments. To employ
these different methods of innovation, someone has to choose which
projects or parts of projects get executed inside, which get executed
outside, and, if outside, by a commercial lab, a university, or a crowdsourcing platform.

These options are referred to, both here and elsewhere in the book
as channels. Webster defines a channel as "a way, course, or direction
of thought or action." These channels will be courses of action leading
to innovation. Much like distribution channels give producers a choice
of how their product is distributed, innovation channels are the
choices by which innovation skills are accessed, and apply to both
internal efforts as well as external ones. As the whole notion of open
innovation has flourished, there have been few attempts to provide
practitioners with a concrete set of guidelines for how and when to
select an innovation channel. At the conclusion of this chapter may be
found a brief discussion of existing business literature on the topic and
will provide you with sources for establishing a deeper foundation on
the channels themselves and their distinctions.

The objective of this chapter is to classify ten distinct innovation
channels, or mechanisms, both internal, or closed, and external, or
open, by which innovation may be accomplished. Having defined
these ten channels, you are then provided with a set of guidelines for
the conditions under which each would be preferred. These guidelines provide channel selection by establishing for each project module an option of archetypes that characterize that specific module.
This chapter complements the framework established in Chapter 3,
"A New Innovation Framework." Think of it as the lab manual or
practicum for Chapter 3's coverage of theory. As previously stated,
the project modules, or challenges, are each distributed among the

innovation channels. In this way, an overall project could conceivably be derived from the use of all ten, or certainly fewer, innovation channels.

Some of this choice making depends on what "kind" of corporation your company is and, to a considerable extent, on your corporation's culture. For example, an organization dominated by a climate of secrecy is not going to make decisions about innovation channels as boldly as another company, even if it is in the same sector and even if it is making decisions about a similar type of task. That said, such cultures may find themselves disadvantaged as the benefits of "openness" often outweigh the risks associated with greater disclosure and transparency. You will note that for each archetype there is a "most preferred" innovation channel. These were constructed assuming a complete openness to new ways of innovating. However, fallback channels are also highlighted.

Other, sometimes pervasive, corporate culture and policy issues exist when your institution is founded on fundamentally different principles of both mission and organizational design, that is, not-for-profit organizations or government agencies as opposed to commercial corporations. In the case of not-for-profit foundations, their mission is to focus on social good rather than monetary return, which may lead to foundations making choices viewed as incompatible in a profit-seeking environment. Furthermore, because most not-for-profit organizations lack a permanent R&D staff, they are compelled to make innovation decisions differently than a for-profit neighbor. To avoid complicating the problem, assume an open mindedness to open innovation and a striving to some sort of evolving norm of diminished corporate isolation. For the most part, the specific recommendations assume a for-profit commercial venture. The adaptations for other organizational types are relatively straightforward after the process is laid out in detail.

Another objective is to find a way to rationally discuss this topic without a constant referral to the scale of the distributed tasks, even though scale could dominate the selection choices. It may be that, if an entire innovation program, say for the development of a new product, is to be moved through a single innovation channel, the channel choice would be substantially different than if each individual task within that program were to have independent innovation channel selections made for it. For the most part, assume that decisions are made about neither scale extreme—that is, not about the channel for an entire program nor for a single, simple work task. Think of a work module, or challenge, as referenced in Chapter 3; this is a unit of work that can be insourced or outsourced, and later reintegrated into a complete program of new product development, novel services, or governmental and regulatory policy.

# A Channel Decision-Making Tool

The final approach, presented here, was to define seven project archetypes and identify ten innovation channels. Each project archetype was then arrayed with the innovation channels, enabling the prioritization of the most suitable channels for each archetype. From this framework, a table with ten rows was constructed, one for each innovation channel and seven columns, one for each of the project archetypes. The chosen priorities are specified by using harvey balls (all black being most recommended) at the intersection of a given row and column. Where the solid black ball appears, this is the most recommended channel (specified by row) for that given archetype (specified by column). Less solid balls would suggest that this channel be considered after the first choice has failed or is deemed otherwise insufficient. Admittedly, there may be more channels that could be created by dividing the ones chosen or adding the ones overlooked. And not *all* projects are a perfect match to one of the seven archetypes presented. But it should make a good starting point for the projects and channels your organization pursues.

The definitions and details are probably necessary to make complete sense of Table 5.1. However, the table is presented first and then those details are filled in. You can thereby decide the extent to which those details are digested. You might use this to begin the "nuts and bolts" process of project dissection and allocation and or to simply understand the overall framework and use the definition portion of this chapter for reference.

**TABLE 5.1    Decision-Making Matrix for Selecting Appropriate Channels of Innovation Given a Project Modules's Specific Archetype**

° See text for definitions and details. Solid black circles indicate recommendation; partial black circles indicate a circumstantial recommendation; and blanks are not recommended channels.

| Module Archetypes/ Innovation Channels | Archetype A Under the Radar Secrecy | Archetype B The Regulated Recipe Recipe/Regulated | Archetype C Follow the Directions Recipe/ Not Regulated | Archetype D Directed Judgment/Fuzzy | Archetype E A New Way To... Judgment/ Low Risk | Archetype F Explore Problem- Solving Space Judgment/Precise/ Risky | Archetype G Fix MY House Precise/Risky/ Local |
|---|---|---|---|---|---|---|---|
| 1. Internal | ● | | | ◐ | ● | | ● |
| 2. Contract research organization | | ◐ | | | ◐ | | |
| 3. Electronic request for proposal | | ● | ◐ | | ◐ | | |
| 4. Offshoring | | | ● | | | | |
| 5. Crowdsourcing/ ideation | | | | ● | | | ● |
| 6. Crowdsourcing/ reduction to practice | | | | | ◐ | ● | |
| 7. University contracts | | | | ◐ | ◐ | | |
| 8. Consulting | ◐ | | | | ● | | ● |
| 9. Right of first refusal | | | | | | ◐ | |
| 10. Joint venture | | | | | | ◐ | |

# Innovation Channels

The ten channels listed below will cover most situations but are admittedly not all inclusive. No line exists for public-private partnerships, which themselves take on many forms. Further, additional rows could be added to the table by subdividing by funding mechanism. Even internal projects could be funded very differently by corporate proceeds, by taking on additional investors with project equity or by use of social impact bonds. For each, we've assumed the most common funding mechanism. The admitted limitations of a table with 70 cells also serves to illustrate the complexity of these choices in real-world practice. But this structure makes a good starting point and will guide most innovation channel decisions with reasonable efficiency and pragmatism.

## Innovation Channel #1: Internal

Just as you would expect, this refers to innovating using the existing resources, namely people and equipment, within an organization. It's the familiar "closed innovation" that required no name until open opportunities became more prevalent.

## Innovation Channel #2: Contract Research Organization (CRO)

CROs usually focus on a well-defined range of specialties and capabilities. Examples of companies, and one example of the services they provide, would include Applied Analytical, which provides active pharmaceutical ingredient stability testing, Covance Labs, which provides toxicology studies, and Probion Analysis, which provides surface and solid state sample characterization. In many instances, they repeat a given type of research more frequently than a product innovator does. This gives them a competitive edge for conducting such studies. An agricultural chemistry innovator that markets specialized crop treatments might perform a certain environmental test one time for each of the three or four products that enter a later stage of research each year. On the other hand, a contract lab specializing in that same study might perform hundreds each year. Engagement with a CRO usually occurs after negotiating a contract.

## Innovation Channel #3: Electronic Request for Proposals, e-RFP

Although the tasks will be carried out in this channel by a traditional research services unit—that is, a contract lab or a university—the contracting organization is identified via an electronic request for proposals. This enables the contracting group to access organizations they may be unaware of and to expand the range of alternatives prior to selection and agreement of terms. This channel is distinguished from the familiar RFP, or call for bids, which could be lumped in with the CRO channel, #2. At first glance it seems to be an artificial divide. Isn't it just a matter of scale? However, as often heard in the complexity sciences, "more really is different." There have been recent, unique service providers in this arena, for example, Nine Sigma, that have helped expand the search so significantly via the Internet that they enable many new connections and enhance the innovation network in ways that didn't exist in historic "bidding."

## *Innovation Channel #4: Off-Shoring*

The distinctions between this channel and the CRO, channel #2, may also seem a bit contrived, but it is useful to recognize that for certain types of tasks, there is a legitimate motivation to get it done at a low cost. This rationale is usually captured by the term **off-shoring** versus **outsourcing**, because the off-shoring most often refers to the placement of the work in countries where labor costs are significantly lower. A variation within this channel is illustrated by the company oDesk, a business that assembles workers around the world to engage in tasks that can be fully digitized and communicated via computer connections. This straightforward means of engagement reduces not only the direct labor costs but also reduces the transaction costs of contracting and negotiating.

## *Innovation Channel #5: Crowdsourcing, Ideation*

Many times the innovation channel described here, and in channel #6, as "crowdsourcing" is *not* divided into subcategories. This channel is subdivided because some types of crowdsourcing are more appropriate to some archetypes than other types of crowdsourcing. Channel #5 refers to the broadcasting of challenges to a wide audience but with the expectation that the solving audience would respond with only their ideas or a theoretical justification for why their approach should work. This ideation effort can be as simple as the "jams" that have been popularized to broadly solicit ideas, a global brainstorming if you will. Or it can be as complex as proposed new mechanisms for disease treatment requiring exhaustively cross-referenced research papers. Either way, the important distinction from #6 is that Channel #5 does not require anything by way of equipment or laboratory facilities; its work product is primarily intellectual in nature.

## Innovation Channel #6: Crowdsourcing/Reduction to Practice

This second crowdsourcing channel assumes that the solving community will also conduct the studies required for "reduction to practice." The solving community members to whom the challenge is broadcast are expected to conduct appropriate experiments and demonstrate the viability of their solutions. Sometimes the act of "reducing to practice" requires enormous resources—think of the Ansari X Prize in which the submitters had to "build and launch a spacecraft capable of carrying three people to 100 kilometers above the earth's surface, twice within two weeks!"[1] (Exclamation point added, duly.) Usually "reduction to practice crowdsourcing" requires far more modest resources—for example, the Challenges typically posted on InnoCentive. And, sometimes the resources are little different from the tools required to access the Challenge—for example, the creation of computer code for an open source software package or for an algorithmic challenge posed by Topcoder. (That is, the very tool by which you accessed the website, your computer, can probably, with some software additions, provide you with the laboratory under which you can solve the problems posed.)

## Innovation Channel #7: University Contracts

This channel is considered distinct from either of the outsourcing channels associated with CROs or off-shoring for a variety of reasons.

The work is often conducted as part of graduate student thesis efforts, with special IP and publication issues, and more important, the efforts themselves provide affiliation with some of the most respected and trustworthy brands in the world: Harvard, Stanford, INSEAD, and so forth. These distinctive characteristics of academia are a part of why this channel may be chosen, under what conditions it is appropriate, and how results should be managed.

### Innovation Channel #8: Consulting

Other than the channel for internal innovation, this may be the channel with the longest history and is self-explanatory.

### Innovation Channel #9: Right of First Refusal

"Right of first refusal," seems less of an innovation channel than a contract term. Admittedly true. But it offers a unique way to manage risk—by paying for "fewer" rights upfront in exchange for the right to negotiate for greater IP, at a later date, after risks have been reduced by experimental outcomes. For this reason, it should be made part of explicit decision making and not treated as a contractual after-thought.

### Innovation Channel #10: Joint Venture

This channel is usually employed when entities, which usually do not compete with each other, may both benefit from the outcomes of an innovation endeavor and want to share risks, costs, and of course, financially attractive outcomes. It is used historically to enter new geographies—often combining one firm's knowledge of the local market with another's knowledge of the technology. It is used too infrequently for portfolio management and balancing. It offers a chance for constrained budgets to explore more alternatives as costs are split between two partners. Yes, rewards have to be shared also—and this is sometimes dissuasive. But by sharing uncertain outcomes across more projects, the expected value of the portfolio can usually be realized with its variance being simultaneously reduced.

To define each archetype as succinctly as possible, some terms need to be introduced along with existing descriptors in a specific way. Each of the terms used in constructing the archetypes, which identify the central characteristics of different types of problems, are defined.

# Terms Used in Defining Archetypess

**Secrecy:** There are circumstances in which the project's solution and the solving techniques *must* be confidential. In addition, sometimes reasons exist for avoiding even the disclosure that this product or project is of interest; that is, you don't want anyone, and especially competitors, knowing what you are working on, or whether you are close to a solution. The innovation channels must be chosen to minimize exposure.

**Recipe:** Certain tasks, in an overall innovation endeavor, may be characterized by the presence of a "recipe" that can be followed. The presence of a recipe does not preclude that it is being applied to something of an incredibly ingenious nature. Even a breakthrough cure for cancer needs to be shown to be stable under anticipated storage conditions. That stability measurement may follow a tightly prescribed protocol or recipe.

**Regulated:** Many research tasks fall under the regulatory purview of professional societies, or, most often, government agencies. In those cases, special consideration must be given not only to HOW tasks are carried out but at times even by WHOM. Some regulators require certification of the individuals, labs or institutes conducting the work.

**Judgment:** This is a task in which no recipe can be followed. It is something that may require points of judgment and complex choice making, usually predicated on some level of expertise or ingenuity. This would also include efforts for which invention must occur on the project's critical path.

**Fuzzy:** Unfortunately defies attempts at description. Some project tasks have a well-defined outcome, describable in advance, whereas others fall into the old category of "I'll know it when I see it." It is these latter types of investigations that are called fuzzy.

**Precise:** This doesn't refer to the integrity or degree of the measurements but to the specifiability of the outcome. Can you describe, precisely, what that outcome will look like even before it is actually known? This term is used in opposition to the term fuzzy.

**Risky:** Risky projects are those that have a low probability of success but which require substantial resources for resolution. These two elements, probability and expense, play off one another. For example, the lower the expense for resolution, the lower probability of success you can tolerate. In other words, if you're not spending much money, if you're not "at risk," you can accept that the likely outcome is failure. A project that doesn't require extraordinary resources and is likely to succeed in a relatively few number of attempts is defined as low risk.

Another way to look at risky projects would be to realize that their "solution surface" is rugged, complex, and difficult to explore. A solution surface is defined as the goodness of outcome for any given experiment involving the adjustment of multiple experimental parameters. If the optimal solution, or near-optimal solution, must be found on that surface, the project is likely high risk. If the surface is scattered with many "good enough" solutions, the project is likely low risk.

**Local:** Although all projects require some sort of domain knowledge, that is, computer programming, engineering, physics, compensation strategies, bookkeeping, and so on, they may not require knowledge specific to the seeker's environment. However, some solutions are useful *only* when they comply with the demands of a specific environment, an environment not easily replicated elsewhere.

# Project Module Archetypes

With the project elements defined, you can now combine these specific terms to create the archetypes and discuss which channel is appropriate for each and which channels may act as fallback positions, owing to nuances of the project or failure to achieve results on first attempts. The text that describes each of the archetype scenarios can serve to clarify what you can probably already infer from a studious examination of Table 5.1.

### Archetype A: "Under the Radar" Descriptors: Secrecy

The first archetype is dominated by the need for secrecy. That need trumps other project properties and almost solely determines channel selection. In this instance, it is important not only that the solution and the approach to problem solving be kept confidential but also that the problem and the organization's pursuit of a solution is confidential. An example might be a decision to investigate and commercialize a new technology.

The authors issue a caveat: Confidentiality is *often* used as a rationale for explaining why a company cannot more fully engage in the use of open innovation. This is more often than not a retreat to territory that is hard to debate. The need for confidentiality is often over-fretted about and overstated. The reality is that far less is disclosed than you might imagine. What seems obvious to the people working intently on a given approach is actually much less obvious to even domain experts who are not actively pursuing that particular approach. Although hard to actually quantify in practice, it is difficult, based on the authors' research experience, to imagine that any more than ten percent of the tasks undertaken actually belongs to this archetype.

When secrecy does dominate, and this is the appropriate archetype to consider, using internal resources is the channel of choice. If it is necessary to involve those outside the organization, then the fewer involved, the better. For this reason, a secondary channel would be consulting, where disclosure is limited, often times to one person, and at most, usually a small handful.

## Archetype B: "The Regulated Recipe" Descriptors: Recipe, Regulated

The second archetype is one for which there is external regulation and for which it is appropriate to employ a recipe, a protocol that can readily be followed by reasonably trained workers. A good example would be stability studies carried out on new pharmaceutical agents.

The most appropriate channel to use for project modules fitting this archetype is a contract research organization. In this circumstance, a CRO is chosen because its tendency to specialize makes it better prepared to deal with regulatory requirements. Also the frequency with which the CROs execute specialized studies enables them to more appropriately respond to regulatory queries. We have shown a preference for the electronic request for proposal (e-RFP) preceding the CRO engagement because the number of available and properly skilled CROs is usually much greater than any organization's regular list of CRO contacts. The use of the e-RFP may also enable the seeker to find the most appropriate overlap of individual and unusual skill sets.

## Archetype C: "Follow the Directions" Descriptors: Recipe, Not Regulated

The third archetype resembles the second in that a protocol is available to which the execution tasks can adhere. But it differs from the second archetype because there is no regulatory oversight. An example would be a standardized test of tensile strength or the preparation of circuit board prototypes. Thus the emphasis is on the quality of the results, as opposed to the regulatory-mandated activities inherent in the procedure. It is also less crucial that the organization conducting the study be well known to regulatory authorities or that its track record has been proven, or that an audit trail needs be rigorously established if future inspections occur. This relaxing of regulatory concerns can enable you to be more sensitive to costs and less sensitive to reputation. The preferred channel for this archetype is off-shoring.

Where the work being conducted requires some specialized facility, a contractual relationship with an offshore partner is usually best. Where the work requires no specialized facility and can be done "from home," then a distributed work system such as oDesk[2] is appropriate. As an alternative, the use of an e-RFP process is recommended although that process will be used primarily to find appropriately low cost providers. If the need were significant for novel approaches, in-progress judgments, or rare capabilities, a different archetype would have been assigned.

### Archetype D: "Directed Stumbling" Descriptors: Judgment, Fuzzy

The fourth archetype is characterized first by the *absence* of a recipe that may be followed. It requires that you make judgments as the work evolves, and at times you need to achieve full-out, inline invention. An example might be a business plan definition or finding a new electricity conducting polymer. Archetype D is further focused on those projects for which the outcome may not be declared clearly in advance—for which the outcome is fuzzy. Over the course of work on such a project, new ideas will be generated and tested, and a solution will emerge without having been predefined. This is the project challenge where you will know the answer when you see it, and much stumbling around will occur enroute to that answer.

The first channel of choice for this archetype is to crowdsource an idea or a theoretical solution. The use of ideas and theoretical solutions minimizes the overall degree of wasted effort and enables the project owner to try out many possibilities before selecting one that appears to offer promise. Crowdsourcing also enables these multiple approaches to be proposed in parallel, and with the appropriate reward structures enabling the ultimate benefactor to pay only for what seems promising and to not pay for the dead-end ventures, which are inevitable when a project has that "stumbling around," fuzzy quality.

As a backup to the crowdsourcing approach, again the use of internal resources that enable you to iteratively "stumble around" and ask, "Does this look promising?" is recommended.

A third channel of choice might be contracting with a university research group. Such open-ended endeavors are more valued in the academic environment, not only for the graduate student training ripe within, but also, the ability to spawn future avenues of research, which may, in some cases, not be viewed as competitively advantageous by the commercial grant provider.

### Archetype E: "A New Way To..." Descriptors: Judgment, Precise, Low Risk

The fifth archetype shares that need for judgment with the fourth archetype. But in this archetype, the nature of the solution *can* be defined in advance. A good example of a solution that can be defined in advance would be seeking a means of fusing two different materials together. You are likely to succeed, but the task could still require several judgments and the solid material at the end is a clear indicator of success. And finally, this archetype is characterized as being low risk.

Because this archetype is characterized by low risk—and hence calls for a somewhat straightforward application of the appropriate skill sets—the first choices of innovation channels are internal execution, assuming the internal organization is still packed with domain experts, and engagement of a skilled consultant. These channels enable the seeking organization to identify the skill sets required to solve the problem and apply them efficiently. If there are other considerations like capacity, that is, "We just don't have time to do it ourselves," then CROs, either with or without an electronic request for proposals, may be used.

As a third priority, many universities are willing to engage in low-risk execution where the requirement for judgment can be beneficial in the training of students. And also as a third priority, may be the option to crowdsource a reduction to a practice solution. In this instance, the diversity associated with crowdsourcing may not be demanded for the exploration of solution space but rather to sample a variety of judgments, all likely leading to the desired outcome. Crowdsourcing may also be uniquely advantageous where the low transaction costs associated with engaging "a crowd" are more attractive than the higher transaction costs associated with negotiating and contracting with universities and CROs.

### Archetype F: "Explore Problem-Solving Space"
### Descriptors: Judgment, Precise, Risky

The sixth archetype, like the fifth, will also require judgment during execution and possesses a precisely defined outcome. But the likelihood of arriving at a satisfactory answer is low. Thus, this is a "risky" endeavor. An example might be to develop a new chemical synthesis—the target molecule being defined precisely, while the intermediate molecular structures and processes are entirely open-ended and subject to extremely complex rules of selection, and even intuitive leaps. In this instance, the clearly preferred channel is to crowdsource with a demonstrated reduction to practice. That serves not only to tap a crowd's diversity but to offload the execution risk and the likely potential for technical failure.

Here the diversity of the crowd enables solution space to be widely sampled in parallel, ensuring that the overall investigation does not bog down on the necessity of conserving resources and having encountered an area of solution space that looks deceivingly encouraging.

As a fallback, the use of joint ventures is recommended, where expenses and risks are shared. As a final option, contracting is suggested, under terms where the cost of failure can be minimized by purchasing only a right of first refusal up front.

It is not recommend that risky ventures be conducted solely in-house, although they usually are. In that case, the costs associated with failure are borne exclusively by the investigating organization. And the domain biases—which come with expertise, as explained in Chapter 4, "The Long Tail of Expertise,"—constrain the ability to effectively search broadly for solutions.

### Archetype G: "Fix MY House" Descriptors: Judgment, Precise, Risky, Local

The seventh, and final, archetype contains all the elements present in the sixth—judgment, outcome precision, and riskiness, plus a fourth element: local knowledge. The demand for local knowledge is a substantial constraint on the use of open innovation channels because that local knowledge is intrinsic only to the closed channel—by definition. This archetype is appropriate when you need to know the specific characteristics of a niche customer base to improve service or the exact configuration of the production line to fix a problem that has arisen or where the presence of domain knowledge becomes of vanishing importance. So, in spite of the adverse consequences of centrally holding the risk and paying for all the likely failures, it is necessary to once again recommend internal research as the preferred channel. Some diversification can be achieved by engaging consultants on-site where they may quickly come up to speed for the local conditions and unique configurations that the solution must address.

A final alternative for this archetype, on par with internal efforts under some conditions, is to consider crowdsourcing solutions in a way that acknowledges the inability to disclose the local knowledge, but at least widely explores the applicability of domain knowledge. This last alternative channel is a reminder that there are times when your failure to solve a local problem is, actually, a failure to explore all the realms of domain knowledge that might be brought to bear on that local problem.

As acknowledged earlier, the channel recommendations are undoubtedly incomplete; though, a practical and practicable middle ground is presented. On the one hand, you need to consider enough elements of a decision to differentiate among an increasing number of innovation channel options. At the same time, you must narrow your selection criteria to few enough elements so that the problem does not combinatorially "explode" without a concurrent increase in utility.

Can you find a particular need that doesn't fit one of the archetypes? Probably. Can you find a particular channel that doesn't fit those described? Probably. But if you can cover 80 percent or 90 percent of the real-world situations, then you will have accomplished your task. The seven archetypes and the ten channels can provide guidance for the few examples that do not fit within this construct— and at the same time, an understanding of the principles involved in arriving at this formulation can also enable you to make adjustments, as necessary, to fit a future circumstance.

As covered in the overview, this chapter was directed to the project leaders, the department supervisors, and the technologists, artists, and scientists charged with making innovation actually happen. The recommended channels are best for the unit of work that has been modularized and defined. But, practice also invokes a larger benefit for the organization at large. A portfolio of innovation projects, properly channeled will produce the risk management and overall improved organizational performance argued for many times in this text.

But these channel recommendations hardly stand in strict isolation. One important paper touching on topic of multiple channels, and choosing between them, was published in 2008 by Roberto Verganti and Gary Pisano at Harvard Business School; the paper includes an outstanding analysis of selected channel categories, clusters of channels that share properties of openness or closedness, and flat or hierarchal authority structures. Verganti and Pisano define these categories and their distinctive properties and applications.[3] The following year, Eric Bonabeau published a excellent piece on "Decisions 2.0," in the *Sloan Management Review*. That work categorizes open platforms according to type of innovation function, types of questions asked, and explores the important issue of diversity versus expertise.[4] And in 2010, Carliss Baldwin and Eric von Hippel, examined three basic modalities of innovation: single user (imagine designing a custom inline skateboard for yourself); producer (the most classic approach, an innovation arising primarily from a closed system and made available for sale by the innovator); and open collaboration (the most familiar instance being open-source software). The three modalities were linked by a mathematical model that allowed the viability of each to be assessed across a matrix of communication costs (the costs of sharing and exchanging information) and design costs (the costs of coming up with something unlike the current choices).[5] For all innovators, these works are to be highly recommended and the real-world impact of professor Pisano's analysis are an integral part of the NASA case study at the end of Chapter 3.

# The Challenge Driven Enterprise

At this halfway point in the book, you have learned predominantly about why, and in what way, a highly connected future can alter your innovation processes. Chapter 2, "The Future of Value Creation," noted that the changes in store for innovation were predicated upon the design logic of the firm and that vertical disintegration was not limited to innovation functions. Chapter 3 telegraphed some of ways in which the internal innovation activities and roles need to change, under a different framework for innovation and the management of distributed projects. The subsequent chapters focus more on the broader organizational changes and the processes necessary to better compete in the flat world. You see the shift from Challenge Driven Innovation to the organizational strategies and practices that can best achieve it: the Challenge Driven Enterprise.

## Case Study: How Eli Lilly and Company Is Changing from a Closed Company to an Open Network to Provide Medicines for the Twenty-First Century

At a Brookings Institution Conference in 2010, keynote speaker John Lechleiter, Eli Lilly's CEO and Chairman, stated:

> The Lilly I joined as a scientist over 30 years ago was a 'fully integrated pharmaceutical **company**'—or FIPCo—that owned the entire value chain from an idea in a researcher's lab to a pill in a patient's medicine chest. As we entered the 21st century, Lilly adopted a new model—a 'fully integrated pharmaceutical **network**.' This FIPNet still stresses the integration aspect...with Lilly assembling and orchestrating the network...but more and more of the pieces are linked through partnerships, alliances, and other relationships and transactions...rather than always through outright ownership. A well-developed FIPNet allows us to cast a wider net—for ideas, for molecules, for talent, and for resources. In the process, we can greatly expand the pool of opportunity. We can leverage our financial resources by sharing investment, risk, and reward. This wider net is global; so, not surprisingly, we're doing more work in China and India, tapping into the vast intellectual capital in those countries.
>
> —*John C. Lechleiter, PhD*
>    *Chairman, President and Chief Executive Officer,*
>    *Eli Lilly and Company*[6]

Now rewind the clock a few years. The moniker FIPCo for Fully Integrated Pharmaceutical Company arose in the late 1990s. It served both to define what the largest companies in the pharmaceutical industry were—and what they were not. It was a distinction—and one that you could be proud of. FIPCos did it all: from the discovery of drug candidates, to their development, to their manufacturing, to their marketing, to their sales and delivery. Biotechs were useful; but, if their products were going to reach patients, they were either sold to a FIPCo or the biotech "grew up" into a FIPCo, such as the legendary Genentech and Amgen.

At Eli Lilly & Co., all the executives understood the value of being a FIPCo and what that meant. But as a strategic intention, it fell short. It didn't differentiate Lilly from its competitors and, as the world changed, it seemed less relevant. FIPCos were relying on biotechs to source new pipeline candidates. On the other end of the spectrum, they were contracting sales forces to generate revenue. Recognizing the degree to which key strategic decisions deviated from the organizational framework of a FIPCo, Lilly coined the term FIPNet, meaning Fully Integrated Pharmaceutical Network, suggesting the merits of the integrated process but acknowledging that it could be a network, not a single corporate entity. Actually, that it *should* at some point in the future be a network—for reasons of better managing a risky business and ensuring continued advancements by attracting resources and ideas from around the world. As this notion was unpacked, it began to not only better address a changing world, but was also a source of freedom in the way organizational structures and capabilities were accessed.

By the year 2006, when the term FIPNet came into corporate usage, the transformation from a "Co" to a "Net" was already underway. Lilly had realized that drug development efficiency was hampered by the high ratio of fixed to variable costs and had begun changing this. Lilly executives realized that they had to attract external s and had "spun out" entities like *InnoCentive* (a crowdsourcing model for complex problem solving) and *YourEncore* (in partnership with Procter & Gamble, a consulting firm providing specialized resources for a retiree population), while creating new *internal* capabilities to orchestrate the *external* work, such as *Chorus*—which worked externally to develop clinical study designs and protocols and then orchestrated their execution by external research centers.

According to Peter Johnson, Lilly's VP of Strategy, "The FIPCo (Fully Integrated Pharmaceutical Company) was a description of the past. It lacked a visionary component, and the world was changing too fast. Every time we felt that we had made a smart, adaptive move, it seemed 'anti-FIPCo.' We needed a simple concept that provided strategic alignment and a 'northstar' for choice making. Becoming a FIPNet (Fully Integrated Pharmaceutical Network), even as the term was in the process of being defined, allowed many executives to make distinctions and work in greater harmony. It meant some divestitures made sense; it meant that contracting had a real role alongside hiring. It also meant that external talent needed to be nurtured just as internal talent did—that renting sometimes made more sense than owning. Finally, it meant that, at times, orchestration trumped management as a tool for getting stuff done."

Since the strategic declaration that it would "orchestrate the Fully Integrated Pharmaceutical Network" as opposed to "build and maintain the Fully Integrated Pharmaceutical Company," Lilly has taken many bold steps toward the realization of that goal. In 2007, Lilly divested the entire toxicology function. Toxicology is the study of the bodies response to introduced chemical substances, whether they originate in the food chain, environmental sources, or the medicines used to treat disease. This wasn't simply following the adage, "Sell the mailroom." Toxicology, as a crucial R&D capability, had long been viewed as core to the company's operations and a strategic advantage. But now, that view was seen as right for a different era. There never was and never would be unanimous agreement in favor of such a radical step; good arguments abound on both sides. But the truth was that as contract services and marketplaces in complex medicinal research functions became more and more available and globalized, some capabilities were more efficiently contracted (and sustained) externally. And the FIPNet vision helped in making the call.

The transformation continues to this day. In 2010, it was reported that Lilly and other partners would create up to $750 million in various external venture capital funds to identify new drug candidates and develop them through clinical proof of concept. Lilly would directly invest up to $50 million in each of three geographically distinct funds as a 20 percent contributor. Of course, its contributions go way beyond the capital infusion. Its tacit know-how for drug development and the capabilities of development platforms such as Chorus[7] could make the productivity of these funds more impressive than their size alone.

It won't be easy for other companies to follow this network model. Years of managerial development do not necessarily produce the essential skills of orchestration. And the organizational and cultural challenges are daunting. The divestiture of functions, the retraining of individuals for new ways to work and contribute, and that risk sharing means reward sharing in the end will pose significant barriers. Both vision and courageous leadership will be required to make the jump.

# Part II

## The Challenge Driven Enterprise: Virtualizing the Business Model to Drive Innovation, Agility, and Value Creation

# 6

# The Challenge Driven Enterprise

"Every day you may make progress. Every step may be fruit-ful. Yet there will stretch out before you an ever-lengthening, ever-ascending, ever-improving path. You know you will never get to the end of the journey. But this, so far from discouraging, only adds to the joy and glory of the climb."

—*Sir Winston Churchill in* Painting as a Pastime

## Overview

Imagine every department with a clear picture of its needs, options, and work in process. Imagine each decision being made by managers bound to driving the optimal outcome regardless of where the resources reside. Imagine the vibrancy of an organization whose singular focus is driving performance excellence and not measuring success by patents issued, full-time headcount, or the size of its R&D budget. In such an organization, the CEOs agenda is that of the investor: How can the firm drive the best returns? The CFO not only tracks the business, he also manages risk and opportunity by measuring the effectiveness of all parts of the organization to deliver against its goals—in business and economic terms—with innovation held to the same performance standards as every other part of the organization.

Whether it is marketing, information technology, product development, or manufacturing, every department understands its problems and challenges and its various channels for problem solving, and has the skills to manage the process effectively, take action, and create solutions to drive enterprise value.

Too often organizations measure their success by % of sales spent on R&D, how many patents they own, or whether the leading academics in their fields are on retainer. However, in today's economy, these should all matter much less to the management of the organization or to the shareholders than whether they can get a new product to market before the competition and dominate the category or whether resources are being managed to ensure the firm can aggressively pursue new business opportunities when they emerge. The prevailing mentality of most established businesses slows, if not discourages, innovation while increasing its costs. Ultimately the shareholders pay the price.

Challenge Driven Innovation represents a dramatic evolution in enabling more effective, efficient, and predictable innovation. And our experience with businesses suggests there is enormous benefit simply in managers and employees better defining and managing their own problems. The transformational change, however, is accomplished through the remaking of the organization into the Challenge Driven Enterprise, where the most difficult problems can be solved, effort is aligned with strategic goals, all talent inside and outside of the organization is brought to bear to deliver on the mission, and sustained performance improvement is possible.

The Challenge Driven Enterprise represents a new vision with far-reaching implications that can improve the speed, agility, and efficiency of business. It enables new modes of innovation while creating the flexibility to capitalize on new business opportunities. Industry leaders will be those that successfully apply these concepts universally, from business strategy to the manufacturing plant floor.

Li & Fung Ltd, the Hong Kong-based trading company, vented itself as a highly dynamic virtual company. It provides an outstanding example of the power of this approach (see Li & Fung Case Study in Chapter 2, "The Future of Value Creation") and provides an excellent glimpse into the future. Meanwhile, new firms such as Top-Coder, LiveOps, and InnoCentive are emerging that enable many of the principles outlined in this book. And they are already helping to redefine competitiveness for hundreds of the world's top companies.

This chapter defines a Challenge, explores why it works, discusses mechanisms by which a challenge-based approach can be implemented as a core process, and offers a number of select examples. Then the Challenge Driven Enterprise is formally defined, which provides an end-state vision for organizations to drive innovation, agility, and better economics for doing business in the 21st century.

# What Is a Challenge?

Too many organizations struggle to define their problems and goals, much less to innovate with the precision and efficiency needed to compete in the world today. Whether building better business strategies or designing new technologies to dominate a market, traditional business practices are no longer sufficient. Nowhere is this truer than in large corporations where years of accumulated standard operating procedures, poorly aligned incentives, ever-increasing bureaucracy, and entrenched culture work together to ensure that increasingly expensive and mediocre innovation is the best they can do. The existing systems are failing and firms are in desperate need of new methods to improve responsiveness and competitiveness.

Dictionary.com defines a "challenge" as "a summons to engage in any contest" or as "a job or undertaking that is stimulating to one engaged in it." However, it is much more. Well-constructed "challenges" are an astonishingly powerful and uniquely effective tool for focusing the energies of multitudes of creative, inventive, talented audiences on the important problems facing organizations, nations, and the planet on which we live. These audiences can be employees, customers, partners, and a planet of resources.

The Challenge is core to InnoCentive's business, and its power has been on display now for several years. We see early glimpses of this approach throughout history, well before InnoCentive's founding. Striking examples of its use range from the Longitude Prize offered by British Parliament in the 1700s to the Ortiz Prize that induced Charles Lindbergh to cross the Atlantic. It has been shown to have broad and general applicability. InnoCentive has more experience with Challenges than any organization in the world and provides an intriguing sampling of the potential of Challenges in areas as diverse as business entrepreneurship, life sciences, mathematics, and manufacturing. Challenges can deliver breakthrough strategies or highly technical solutions and apply to every business function and every type of problem, large and small, strategic and tactical. A random sampling of InnoCentive Challenges is provided in Figure 6.1.

But why does it work? We first began to understand the Challenge as a powerful business tool a few short years ago. It was at this time that a number of key concepts were beginning to converge, namely that a Challenge exhibits three important properties. They provide:

- Fundamental unit of problem solving;
- Better way to organize work; and
- Powerful strategy tool.

Taken together, these properties position the Challenge at the center of Challenge Driven Innovation (the process) as well as what we call the Challenge Driven Enterprise (a business underpinned by the process), whether for business strategy, driving operational efficiency, or R&D. Let's explore each of these.

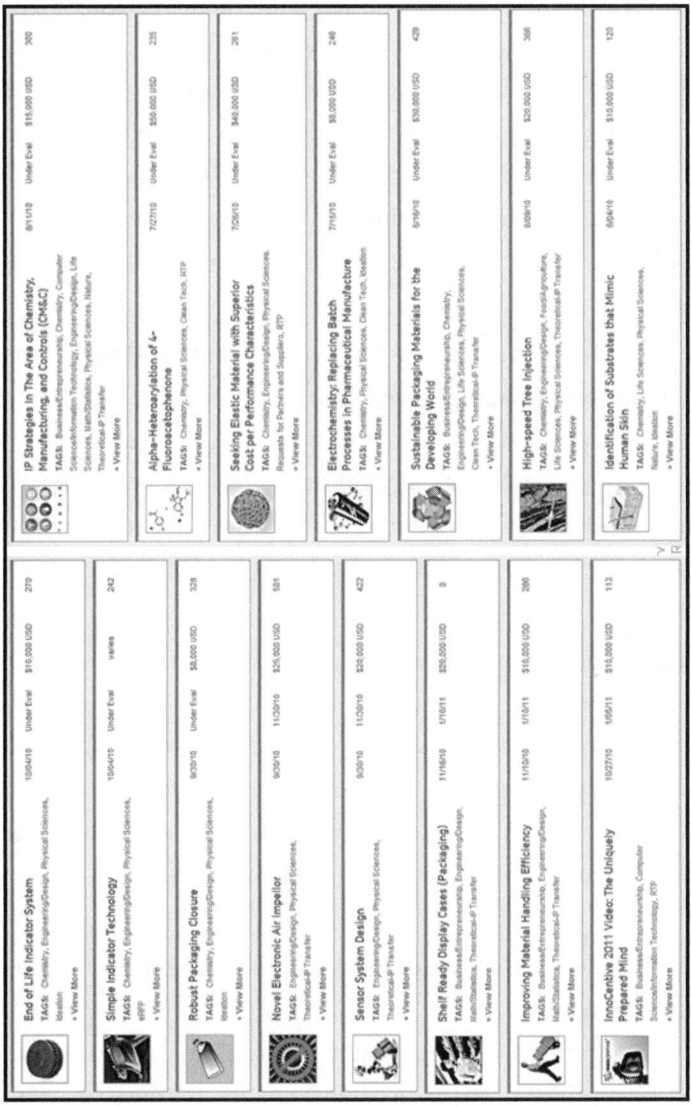

**End of Life Indicator System**
TAGS: Chemistry, Engineering/Design, Physical Sciences, Ideation
10/04/10  Under Eval  $10,000 USD  270
• View More

**Simple Indicator Technology**
TAGS: Chemistry, Engineering/Design, Physical Sciences, eRFP
10/04/10  Under Eval  varies  242
• View More

**Robust Packaging Closure**
TAGS: Chemistry, Engineering/Design, Physical Sciences, Ideation
9/20/10  Under Eval  $8,000 USD  328
• View More

**Novel Electronic Air Impeller**
TAGS: Engineering/Design, Physical Sciences, Theoretical-IP Transfer
9/20/10  11/29/10  $25,000 USD  581
• View More

**Sensor System Design**
TAGS: Engineering/Design, Physical Sciences, Theoretical-IP Transfer
9/20/10  11/29/10  $20,000 USD  422
• View More

**Shelf Ready Display Cases (Packaging)**
TAGS: Business/Entrepreneurship, Engineering/Design, Math/Statistics, Theoretical-IP Transfer
11/16/10  5/15/11  $25,000 USD  0
• View More

**Improving Material Handling Efficiency**
TAGS: Business/Entrepreneurship, Engineering/Design, Math/Statistics, Theoretical-IP Transfer
11/13/10  5/15/11  $10,000 USD  390
• View More

**InnoCentive 2011 Video: The Uniquely Prepared Mind**
TAGS: Business/Entrepreneurship, Computer Science/Information Technology, RTP
10/27/10  5/05/11  $10,000 USD  113
• View More

**IP Strategies in The Area of Chemistry, Manufacturing, and Controls (CM&C)**
TAGS: Business/Entrepreneurship, Chemistry, Computer Science/Information Technology, Engineering/Design, Life Sciences, Math/Statistics, Physical Sciences, Nature, Theoretical-IP Transfer
8/11/10  Under Eval  $15,000 USD  390
• View More

**Alpha-Heteroarylation of 4-Fluoroacetophenone**
TAGS: Chemistry, Physical Sciences, Clean Tech, RTP
7/27/10  Under Eval  $50,000 USD  235
• View More

**Seeking Elastic Material with Superior Cost per Performance Characteristics**
TAGS: Chemistry, Engineering/Design, Physical Sciences, Requests for Partners and Suppliers, RTP
7/26/10  Under Eval  $40,000 USD  281
• View More

**Electrochemistry: Replacing Batch Processes in Pharmaceutical Manufacture**
TAGS: Chemistry, Physical Sciences, Clean Tech, Ideation
7/15/10  Under Eval  $8,000 USD  246
• View More

**Sustainable Packaging Materials for the Developing World**
TAGS: Business/Entrepreneurship, Chemistry, Engineering/Design, Life Sciences, Physical Sciences, Clean Tech, Theoretical-IP Transfer
5/16/10  Under Eval  $30,000 USD  429
• View More

**High-speed Tree Injection**
TAGS: Chemistry, Engineering/Design, Feeding/procedures, Life Sciences, Physical Sciences, Theoretical-IP Transfer
6/08/10  Under Eval  $20,000 USD  366
• View More

**Identification of Substrates that Mimic Human Skin**
TAGS: Chemistry, Life Sciences, Physical Sciences, Nature, Ideation
6/04/10  Under Eval  $10,000 USD  120
• View More

Source: InnoCentive

**Figure 6.1   How InnoCentive Challenges address a multitude of problems**

## I. The Fundamental Unit of Problem Solving

Albert Einstein once famously said "If I were given one hour to save the planet, I would spend 59 minutes defining the problem and one minute resolving it." This provocative statement recognizes the importance of understanding the context of a need, articulating requirements clearly, and applying precision in defining outcomes and goals. Stephen Shapiro, a popular writer and public speaker on the topic of innovation, reflecting on Einstein's words added that in fact "Most companies spend 60 minutes of their time finding solutions to problems that just don't matter." Shapiro's observation is true more than most would admit.

All problems, big or small, must be clearly defined and tied to the strategic goals of organizations. Are some problems too big? Quite the contrary. We have learned at InnoCentive that for the big problems, it is essential to systematically refine them into more focused questions and ultimately to well-defined Challenges. Nearly any outcome focused activity may be cast as a well-defined Challenge or system of Challenges.

Focusing the energy of organizations and even an entire human population on problem solving has always been possible but requires process and tools to do so effectively and at scale. And generally the approaches employed by business have been uneven and imprecise. Rigorous and disciplined construction of Challenges focuses that human energy to drive results in ways never before possible.

Harvard Business School Professor Karim Lakhani and others have consistently confirmed the critical importance of defining the problem, the key to InnoCentive's challenge-based model and its success. The problems must invite diverse participation because you want potential solutions for engineering problems to come not just from engineers, but from entrepreneurs, mechanics, and chemists. At the same time, potential problem solvers must be focused on the specific task at hand with as much context as possible. As you can imagine, getting this right is incredibly important to sustaining high solution rates.

Paul Carlile is a professor from Boston University with an unusual background in both social and computer science and a gift for seeing the world through a system's lens. In 2009, Paul introduced InnoCentive and the authors to the concept of Boundary Objects,[1] which sociologists use to describe powerful compartments of information that are both well defined and that translate naturally across communities and cultures. Examples of boundary objects, discussed briefly in Part I of the book, in the real world would include Laws and Contracts, well defined by their very nature, universally understood, and vital to modern society. InnoCentive Challenges are boundary objects in every sense of the term. Challenges articulate the need, describe the problem, specify success criteria, and establish the inducements. The inducement is a critically important component because it telegraphs a tangible and measurable value to the world. The best Challenges are universal and thus universally understood.

It is the precision and care taken to define the Challenges that elevate them to the status of true boundary objects. A hallmark is the understanding of how to manage the process to truly engage a highly distributed network and focus them to drive successful outcomes. Well-defined Challenges must ask the right questions. Practitioners must be meticulously attentive to detail or else they cannot understand and articulate problems in a concise way. Well-defined Challenges anticipate the audience and the conditions for effective engagement. Does the Challenge call for a new idea or a new business plan? Is the Challenge seeking scientific discovery or simply new approaches? Do you want the world to give you the idea or do you want someone to demonstrate something physical? Challenges must also anticipate the cultural and legal realities of the world (for example, is intellectual property an issue?).

It is important to note that a significant amount of the effort spent on creation, invention, and strategy in many organizations today is wasted, lacking any real precision or definition. How many IT programs over the years lose their original focus and suffer from scope re-definition to the point they look nothing like the original intent? Nor can they be tied to key drivers of the business—and we wonder how that happened. How many marketing programs fail to define measurable analytics and resist any attempt at defining ROI? How many strategies and new product initiatives are undertaken due to the charisma of the sponsor or the allure of a sexy new space rather than a critical assessment of the opportunity, feasibility of approaches, clear statement of success criteria, benefits, and risks? How many R&D programs have no discernable business sponsorship or tie to business plans or future revenue and earnings? Disappointingly, most of our firms are not operating with this precision or clarity.

In his famous speech on May 25th, 1961, President Kennedy said "I believe that this nation should commit itself to achieving the goal, before this decade is out, of landing a man on the moon and returning him safely to Earth." He was challenging a country to put a man on the moon in 10 years, a seemingly impossible task, but one that united a people. Organizations focused on exceedingly well-defined goals, coupled with innovative empowerment structures, will enable stunning outcomes inside and outside of traditional management paradigms.

## II. A Better Way to Organize Work

There are many kinds of work. There's work on the assembly line, analyzing water for impurities, delivering newspapers, and fighting wars. And loosely speaking, Challenges may have a role to play in all these kinds of activities. And there is a different kind of more intellectual work requiring more creativity and invention, whereby a need is identified and a solution sought. Examples include development of a marketing strategy, a new plastic material for manufacturing, or an innovative approach to engaging customers. In this latter kind of work, well-defined challenges represent a powerful tool for organizing human activity and motivating innovative outcomes.

Organizations have spent years defining efficient organizational forms, writing Standard Operating Procedures (SOPs), crafting job descriptions, and even developing robust platforms for planning and tracking work. And they are becoming more efficient. Use of contract labor and outsourcing of work, even whole functions, is more commonplace than ever. These approaches have often improved the bottom lines of businesses by increasing flexibility, lowering costs, and enabling projects to be accelerated. However with notable exceptions, these exercises in efficiency and shifting labor costs have done little to fundamentally change the rules of the game—to create anything like a "step change" in business performance and breakthrugh innovation. In most instances, the 20th-century approach is essentially institutionalized resource planning and labor arbitrage that is simply commoditizing work and trading high cost labor for lower cost alternatives. It is not creating a unique competitive advantage. And it is certainly not tapping the creative capacity of organizations and the world to innovate. In some cases, it has actually achieved the opposite effect. Consider how many companies arguably lost their innovative edge by focusing so singularly on cost reduction that they lost the very resources and capabilities needed to be competitive over time (for example, Dell, General Motors). Some even created their next-generation competition by turning their suppliers and partners into the only true sources of innovation (for example, semiconductor). Clearly a less simplistic and more intriguing model for remaining both competitive and innovative must exist.

If you are to fundamentally transform the economics of businesses, while achieving heightened levels of innovation performance, it is clear that a substantially more scalable approach will be required.

Such an approach would leverage network efficiencies, better economics, and modern technology. Organizations will open up their processes, inviting in thousands or millions of individuals and organizations to participate in their business processes.

Thanks to the Internet, you can now engage a global platform in your problem solving and use this platform to deliver against your goals with precision and consistency, while better leveraging your in-house resources.

But how can you engage this nearly unbounded marketplace of knowledge workers, creative and inventive minds, and productive capacity? You need a robust mechanism of engagement. It must be lightweight. It must be simple. It must be enormously flexible. It must be universally understood. Again, the "Challenge" fills that role, meeting all these requirements. In effect, the Challenge uniquely represents the enabling capability, the universal language, and the rules of engagement in neutral terms in order to empower a truly "open" access to human capital inside and outside the organization. It is magnificent in its simplicity. And in many respects, it has been hiding in plain sight for generations.

What is the inducement to this network of potential problem solvers to answer the call? For a simple idea, a small reward or inducement may be sufficient, whereas a technological innovation may require a team to spend months of time and capital to develop a winning solution, requiring substantial incentives. Internally focused challenges may reward employees with reputation, points for the company store, or lunch with the CEO. Inducements may be peer recognition or once-in-a-lifetime experiences. (InnoCentive and NASA recently offered a unique viewing of a space shuttle launch.) All these things must be assembled into a Challenge before it is exposed to the world of problem solvers. This also enables what some call the transition from Not Invented Here (NIH) to Proudly Found Elsewhere (PFE).

## III. A Powerful Strategy Tool

Modern corporations are expected to design their strategy processes to anticipate the future, identifying new opportunities to drive profits, investing in high return initiatives, disinvesting in low-performing businesses or programs, and ensuring the best returns on capital for shareholders. And some firms do an excellent job of methodically decomposing their broad goals into discrete strategies and tactics and may go even further to define clear measures of success. Done properly, these approaches identify gaps and opportunities for exploitation and prompt the organization to constantly rethink assumptions and model outcomes, and to manage their portfolio of possibilities—all to generate the best business outcomes for stakeholders. This approach to strategy can be highly effective but requires a process discipline and organizational transparency absent in many businesses. It also demands absolute honesty and willingness to look past the status quo, existing power structures, organizational politics, and so on. For a big organization, ignoring these pillars of corporate culture is exceedingly difficult. And therefore, incrementalism and bureaucracy are the organizational norms. The result is that in too many firms, corporate strategy is actually just a form of annual corporate planning in which resources are added or subtracted based upon growth rates and departments' designations as profit or cost centers, or simply to provide justification for increasing or sustaining headcount or budget. A truly challenge-driven approach will shake the status quo to its foundations as its only allegiance is to outcomes and delivering performance excellence. The status quo and existing power structures have no entitlements in a Challenge Driven Enterprise.

Proper strategy requires this absolute transparency and honesty in managing the needs of the organization. By engaging head-on in this process and treating every Challenge as an opportunity to improve the business, organizations link what they do with why they are doing it. There is a top-down and bottom-up triangulation around identified Challenges that is particularly instructive. High-level strategies should be meticulously defined in the language of Challenges, which may be further decomposed as needed. Similarly, new initiatives in lower levels of the organization should be articulated as Challenges, presumably in support of high-level business strategies. By applying a discipline and a rigor, Challenges drive a richer understanding of the business and bring clarity to the prioritization process. Poorly defined Challenges are not likely to support key business strategies. By institutionalizing this approach at all levels of the organization, businesses may better tie activities to strategic goals and in the process foster the development of improved administration and problem solving across the organization. Again, use of a challenge-based approach is good management practice in any event, but should be viewed most importantly as a powerful discipline that enables more effective and open business rather than simply a cost-effective approach to solving problems.

# Hallmarks of the Challenge Driven Enterprise

A great number of behaviors and competencies will describe the Challenge Driven Enterprise, but three in particular distinguish this form from most existing businesses:

- **"Open" Business Model:** Businesses focus their attention on their true core competencies, orchestration and strategy, to deliver against their missions. They orchestrate networks and ecosystems of customers, employees, partners, and markets. These models are highly virtualized in order to maximize innovation, agility, capital flexibility, and shareholder returns. The formation of new businesses and entrants naturally utilize these principles. Established firms must adapt to compete effectively.

- **Talent Management:** Think strategic virtual Human Resource Management. Businesses not only understand, but embrace key trends such as globalization, social networking, generational shifts, and project based work. Further, they recognize the importance of engagement with all their communities and the whole world to drive new ideas, product development, innovation, and even production capacity. This 21st-century evolution of HR makes it more strategic than ever before and vital to the success of the business.

- **Challenge Culture:** Challenges are integrated into the culture at all levels and in all functions. The needs and barriers are well-articulated and, where possible, portable. Executives, managers, and team members are trained and empowered to identify critical problems and issues and to systematically manage these Challenges through to closure for the benefit of shareholders. They can be tackled internally or externally as conditions best dictate. Challenge cultures care only that problems are solved. Who solves them and how is secondary to advancing the business mission every day. Politics, NIH, and bureaucracy are not tolerated and eliminated as inefficient and wasteful. Transparency, process integrity, and measurement are vital and hold accountable all significant projects, initiatives, and investments. Recognition, reward, and promotion systems are aligned. Orchestration skills are evident.

### Early Adoption Is Well Underway

In some areas of the enterprise, some of these concepts may already be in use. To illustrate, look briefly at outsourcing and off-shore software development over the last 20 years. This has been made possible by the development of well-defined rules of engagement and task definition, without which work between individuals and organizations in often different fields and geographies would not be possible. The movement, driven by the need to improve efficiency, has required software developers and managers to go well beyond the structures used in traditional systems development to create universal standards and documentation, modular tasks, and even a systematized management language.

Consider that software application requirements are routinely decomposed into modules, which are in turn assigned to individuals, teams, or individual software development houses. To ensure the right work is completed, a well-articulated design document is developed that acts as the input to the work requested. This document defines in detail the allowable technology on which to build the software, specific behaviors, any appropriate development guidelines, and even specific test cases to ensure the module meets the needs of the overall system to integrate effectively into it. The standards and business processes are so universally accepted that anyone can now engage easily with any development team, onshore or offshore development house. This standardization of business processes and documentation has been a major contributor to the development of India as a powerhouse in low-cost software development. At play here is not simply the development of outsourcing standards, but the realization that complex and mission-critical work may be packaged and deployed in a global economy when, where, and how it is best performed.

A similar story may be told in manufacturing. China, with its low-cost labor resources and now substantial industrial infrastructure, has built an enormous delivery capability in outsourced contract manufacturing. Developed over decades, there are now exceedingly well-defined standards in specifying design, acceptance, and delivery. Contracts and engagement between businesses and contract manufacturers follow standardized processes and templates. Product development and innovation functions have evolved side-by-side with legal and strategic norms in these organizations. Today, any organization that defines its needs can easily access low-cost, high-quality manufacturing capacity overseas—only possible by the clear, unambiguous articulation of needs and requirements. In fact, both software development and contract manufacturing, while specific and special purpose, are highly developed examples of sophisticated Challenges, each of which may be offered, priced, and responded to by hundreds or even thousands of "plug and play" providers.

These are special cases of a Challenge: well-defined require-ments, clear acceptance and performance criteria, linkage to specific needs of the organization. And while operationally focused, they do illustrate that CDE principles are already in use in many contexts. However, organizations must take these concepts much further. The Challenge may be large or small. It can be designed to engage one, ten, or even thousands of individuals or organizations simultaneously. It is constructed with efficiency and effectiveness in mind; and it is not limited to manufacturing or software development activities. It is appropriate for a substantial percentage of work conducted by organ-izations in a modern business context. The Challenge Driven Enter-prise may virtualize 50 percent, 80 percent, or even more of its efforts in the next 10 to 20 years. CDE represents a provocative and ration-ale vision of businesses that enables more open, accelerated, and profitable business than ever before possible. So whether the Chal-lenge to envision a brand-new billion-dollar product line, to out-source manufacturing, or to develop the next-generation technology, the Challenge is fundamental and can efficiently organize business and the world around us.

Consumer products companies are leading the charge in many respects, and they were among the first to invest in and adopt open innovation. The need to stay in front of the competition and to do so consistently has required companies such as P&G to throw away the politics and "Not Invented Here" mentality of the 20th century in favor of engaging the best tools at their disposal, a technique they call Connect + Develop and which you'll read more about in the case study at the end of this chapter.

The CDE approach, adopted pervasively, will require an evolution, if not a revolution, in business architecture. Every aspect of the organi-zation will be engineered to maximize flexibility and access to channels capable of delivering superior results. The Challenge, representing a fundamentally better way to organize work, becomes a key enabler.

## *The Role of Talent Management*

Generally, the talent management function in businesses is managed by the Human Resources department (HR). As the name suggests, Human Resources is not specific to the employees of the company. However, it is clear that is how it developed over time. In the highly dynamic and distributed global market for resources, HR becomes even more strategic to the success of 21st-century organizations, developing the strategies, programs, and tools necessary to deliver on the vision.

HR has always focused on identifying the need for talent in the organization and applying it against a backdrop that includes recruiting, developing, and retaining the best talent. Although the backdrop is still valid, the playing field just grew exponentially (as Figure 4.2 made dramatically clear, HR's new talent accountability is vastly larger than it's historically been). The Talent Management function must go well beyond hiring and firing and compliance with employment regulations, it must now empower and enable all aspects of the Challenge Driven Enterprise. With the Challenge itself playing a pivotal role in defining work, HR is now in a unique position to help transform the organization. As so many mission statements have said "it's about the people." Now, it's about all the people. By working with senior management and the various functional areas of the organization to implement the vision, the enterprise transforms from a hierarchical employee-employer form to a dynamic network structure in which capabilities, processes, and talent channels enable work on a grand scale with unprecedented efficiency. Now HR must anticipate needs across the organization and identify where the talent pools may reside, inside and outside the four walls of the firm, and how best to access them reliably and cost-effectively. It is important to understand that managing a physical workforce is no longer the end goal, rather it is ensuring access to the right talent at the right time for the organization to deliver against its mission. Flexibility and agility must now define this function. And the talent panel is virtually unlimited.

HR leadership must now live up to its name. This is no less a change than the introduction of strategic sourcing and strategic supply chain management into organizations and requires business savvy, effective strategy and execution capabilities, and charismatic leadership. The HR Leader therefore plays as vital as any other member of the senior ranks of the organization. And Boards of Directors can be expected to demand talent management strategies from the CEO and HR leader that show vision, comprehend the complexity and nuance of the business, and anticipate a dramatically changing work environment, and that will scale to ensure long-term competitive advantage. Although often already part of the senior team, the Challenge Driven Enterprise for most organizations will logically precipitate elevation of HR to the C-level suite.

## Leadership and Accountability Play Vital Roles

Challenge Driven Enterprises focus on outcome, assemble and disassemble business lines as needed, and execute with rigor and financial precision. They design their businesses for maximum flexibility, demand open engagement, and make exacting decisions based on the data. This challenge-driven approach will challenge leaders, processes, and culture as they exist today.

You will look at this picture of the future with hesitation and possibly contempt because we imagine leadership as having a deep and profound understanding of the needs of the business today, tomorrow, and the next day. That the fundamental tools and business practices of the past will hold true for the foreseeable future. Tragically, many organizations will misread the tsunami of competitive forces in front of them as the winds of gradual change.

Too often organizations' leadership positions are filled with executives who measure success by the size of their organizations, budgets, and headcount. They keep score by how many factories are managed or how many engineers are under their employ. And senior executives too often convince their CEO and boards of directors that the functions are so different in their industries that normal management techniques do not apply. Innovation is seen as an output of spend. These are all outdated and outmoded notions.

Accounting for the need to indoctrinate the organization with new concepts and tools, every department in every organization should stand ready to justify its approach and expenditures; and failing to do so should result in restructuring with new leadership and work models that distribute work how and where it will be best performed.

Every CEO should be held accountable, and every CEO should hold every leader accountable. Performance excellence and the need for constant innovation are more than aspirations; they are goals that every leader and team member share. Some business will simply require new processes. But in most, the redesign will be more serious, including development of modified business architectures, upgraded skill sets and enhanced competencies, and sometimes bold new leadership. Many organizations, particularly smaller and more recent, will find this approach more natural. Large established organizations may require substantial institutional change.

# The Real Challenge

The toolset described in Part I can be applied to scientific problems, business needs, and even to developing new strategies. When these principles are applied pervasively, the Challenge Driven Enterprise represents an encompassing business vision with far reaching implications. Businesses that adopt this approach will have a unique opportunity to operate more effectively than ever before and to build more flexible organizations with better, faster, and more cost-effective access to an entire world of productive capacity. And will have the flexibility to respond to market opportunities when they arise. Organizations that fail to evolve may face increasing competition by new and emerging competition not saddled by the past.

Make no mistake: This requires significant change in businesses, and the journey will be difficult. Culture becomes entrenched over time, fiefdoms are created, and the status quo sustained and codified in every process, bonus scheme, and hiring plan. Changing that culture to focus on what is important now and truly driving what is in the interest of the shareholder in the long term will not be easy. Only the CEO and the Board of Directors can drive the change needed truly become a CDE, although some successes may be the result of grass roots change. Because change is not easy for organizations, leadership will be crucial.

The remaining chapters go more deeply into the transformation necessary to drive change, put forth a playbook designed for senior leadership to support implementing the Challenge Driven Enterprise, and finally, discuss the kind of leadership requisite to successful transformational change.

# Case Study: How Procter & Gamble Is Innovating Through Connect + Develop

Each year since the early 2000s, P&G asks its businesses, "What consumer needs, when addressed, will drive the growth of your brands?" This perennial exercise—managed by a large team of in-house technology entrepreneurs—is an obvious yet significant step in the ongoing innovation culture P&G lives by called Connect + Develop.

"Reduce wrinkles, improve skin texture and tone." "Improve soil repellency and restoration of hard surfaces." "Create softer paper products with lower lint and higher wet strength."

These layperson descriptions are a part of what P&G dubs a top-ten-needs list, one of which is created annually for each of its businesses by the businesses themselves. All the divisions' top-ten-needs lists together form P&G's uber list, which informs future innovation paths.

Connect + Develop was the strategy to revitalize P&G which, in 2000, self-described its operations as a "mature innovation-based company with rapidly expanding innovation costs, flat R&D productivity, and shriveling top-line growth."

Like so many companies in the 1980s that had moved from a centralized approach to what Bartlett and Ghoshal call the transnational model,[2] P&G woke up in the 21st century to find the competitive landscape had changed dramatically, spurred by technology convergence and the new-styled global economy, in which barriers were lower—or obliterated—and competitors abound. The firm's innovation success rates, the percentage of new products that met P&G's financial objectives, had stagnated at about 35 percent.

A.G. Lafley, the firm's then newly appointed CEO, assessed the business and decided only a radical new approach would bring the company back to its previous stature: Acquire 50 percent of P&G's innovations from outside the company.

The cultural and process transformations required to make this happen were significant if not daunting. For one thing, bench scientists and researchers do not like to be told they are not innovating fast enough, and even the most confident employee might feel a twinge of insecurity about a plan to look externally for good ideas.

But P&G's strategy wasn't to replace the capabilities of "our 7,500 researchers and support staff, but to better leverage them," wrote Larry Huston and Nabil Sakkab in their seminal 2006 HBR article. Better leverage, indeed, is a central theme of the entire Connect + Develop strategy.

Huston was tagged as Connect + Develop's chief architect and driver; however, he firmly contends that the CEO of any organization must make Connect + Develop an explicit company strategy to drive the necessary cultural and business changes.

For P&G, two key factors underpinned its Connect + Develop strategy: First was the belief that finding good ideas and bringing them in-house to enhance and capitalize on internal capabilities was the right approach. It also felt it was crucial to know exactly what it was looking for—customer needs—hence the annual, systematic drafting and honing of the top-ten-needs lists.

Second is P&G's approach around how to tap the vast outside world of innovators to meet its 50 percent target. In a radical move at the time, P&G took a wide view to developing a productive network, scouring the globe for adjacent products and innovations through its network of in-house technology entrepreneurs and its own vast network of suppliers, with its top 15 suppliers representing an estimated 50,000 researchers (in 2006).

Some of its biggest successes in recent years were established through Connect + Develop, including Mr. Clean Magic Eraser, which came from technology licensed from German chemical company BASF, and Swiffer Dusters, adapted from a Japanese competitor called Unicharm Corp. P&G negotiated the rights to sell the product outside of Japan.

Arguably, though, the most innovative aspects of Connect + Develop center on how P&G views and leverages networks beyond its own employees and suppliers using open networks. To complement its proprietary networks, P&G invested in and engages with an entire ecosystem of external partners and networks to source patents, partners, and solutions. For example, as far back as 2000, P&G was an early investor in Yet2.com, which is an online marketplace for intellectual property exchange.

Also in 2000, P&G helped create NineSigma, which crafts technical briefs (succinct problem statements) on behalf of its customers and then sends the briefs to its network of thousands of possible solution providers including individuals, companies, universities, and government and private labs for potential solutions. In 2003, the company, together with Eli Lilly and Company, established YourEncore, now operated independently, which connects a network of 5,000 retired experts with client businesses.

During the past several years, P&G has run dozens of Challenges with InnoCentive (www.innocentive.com), the marketplace pioneering challenge-driven innovation by connecting its Seeker companies who have tough but tractable problems with its global network of nearly a quarter-million expert Solvers who submit their solutions for cash awards.

The next level of P&G's commitment to Connect + Develop is leading the way in developing the infrastructure to systematically measure the value of its open innovation practices.

# 7

# Transformation

"Everybody has accepted by now that 'change is unavoidable.' But this still implies that change is like 'death and taxes': It should be postponed as long as possible, and no change would be vastly preferable. But in a period of upheavals, such as the one we are living in, change is the norm."

—*Peter F. Drucker in* Management Challenges for the 21st Century

## Overview

In the year 2000, as companies were putting the Y2K computer bug behind them and the world was ushering in the new millennium, A.G. Lafley was appointed the new CEO of P&G after several years of disappointing growth. He soon challenged his employees to think differently as he famously announced a bold goal of tapping the outside world for 50 percent of all new ideas and innovations over the next few years in a program that became known as Connect + Develop. In the same year, General Electric CEO Jack Welch said in a letter to shareholders (also signed by Jeffrey Immelt and others) that "Globalization has transformed us into a company that searches the world, not just to sell or to source, but to find intellectual capital—the world's best talents and greatest ideas." These were astounding actions and statements by business leaders of two of the most enduring brands in the world. Although new global realities were certainly affecting businesses in myriad ways, ten years ago few CEOs were trumpeting their organization's efforts to tap a whole new world of talent, resources, and innovation. Lafley and Welch were trailblazers and clearly unafraid to challenge convention, recognizing the need to innovate their business models and in many respects to remake their cultures. And based on the financial performance of their companies, history judged them the right leaders at the right time.

Today, the business landscape is even more challenging—customer expectations have increased, product cycles compressed, and aggressive new competition crowd the marketplace. Businesses are more in need of powerful new approaches than ever. Today's business leaders face unprecedented challenges and they must boldly adapt and evolve their organizations with the same conviction as these leaders did a decade earlier, beginning with an objective assessment of their organization's readiness to compete in coming years.

The need for change and the elevated level of CEO urgency was underscored in the IBM 2008 Global CEO Study,[1] which interviewed more than 1,000 CEOs and public sector leaders. Survey results clearly showed that leaders do not believe their organizations can adapt quickly enough to the changes ahead; and worse, CEOs believe the gap between their readiness and future business challenges is actually widening. In the face of unprecedented competition and accelerating rates of change, our organizations are failing to keep pace.

This chapter discusses the evolution of how modern firms are organized (the "bureaucratic" form) and the evolving "network" form that is replacing it, the powerful role of corporate culture in supporting or resisting the transformation, and finally the intense effort that goes into building a new organizational structure along with key considerations for CEOs and business leaders as they contemplate the change ahead.

# Organizational Forms and the Emergence of a New Paradigm

Arguably, the earliest groups to organize were nomadic tribes, clans, and villages and, in a sense, these were the first organizations. They had a semblance of structure and common purpose: food, security, and some hint at order. Ultimately, some yielding of individual freedom was traded in favor of the collective good. Over time, leadership positions were established with well-defined chains of command and decision making. Eventually, more efficient and complex organizations developed across the spectrum of human interaction, including government, commerce, religion, education, and even professional guilds.

In the modern business context, organizational forms evolved to produce and distribute goods and services at increasingly large scale, which required the coordination of multitudes of highly specialized workers over great distances in order to drive efficiency and orderly execution. Organizational theorists sometimes refer to the modern corporation as the *bureaucratic* form and the twentieth century owes no small amount of its success to its emergence. The bureaucratic form supports and is supported by large numbers of employees, sizable capital and real estate holdings, and considerable investments in operating and technology infrastructures. In addition, there is the formidable weight of decades of accumulated policies, procedures, and corporate culture. Our corporations were designed at a time when sheer scale trumped nearly everything. In actuality, this form was rational both operationally and economically, enabling an unprecedented era of large-scale enterprise.[2]

These scale economies came very often at the high price of creativity, agility, and freedom to operate. As we have streamlined and mechanized our businesses to improve efficiency, we have often driven creativity and experimentation out of the system. As we hired exclusively the top talent from the most prestigious schools, we reduced diversity and non-conventional thinking. As we acquired smaller, more agile companies as sources of new products and innovative energy, we integrated them fully into our bureaucracies and destroyed the very value we were seeking. As we built physical plant, we locked our organizations into specific modes of activity and tied up capital available to exploit new opportunities. And the more we have tried to engineer inventiveness and innovation into the process, the more expensive the endeavor has become.

Many enterprises have spent considerable time and resources blending elements of smaller more agile organizations and decentralized decision making with the bureaucratic form to drive innovative thinking, better action in the field, and improved business agility while maintaining the benefits of scale. These efforts have delivered mixed results. In reality, it is quite difficult to have it both ways.

So why has the bureaucratic form persisted for so long? Firstly, given the high costs traditionally facing new entrants (acquiring talent, building factories, distributing products, etc.), large-scale businesses easily dominated their industries. In many cases, the first to scale was the winner. And secondly, at a certain critical mass, they could simply spend their way into new areas of business and new products. In the last few years, however, everything has changed. The barriers to entry and competition have fallen. New ideas can be developed, products manufactured and distributed, and customers supported on an enormous scale in minimal time at low cost. We have reached the inherent limits of the bureaucratic model as we know it. This is particularly evident in larger established businesses which are bloated and inflexible at precisely the time they need to be virtual and lean. And the financial flexibility needed to rapidly capitalize on new business opportunities is diminished by the sizable investments carried on balance sheets from years of buildup activity. Today many of our most successful corporations and heralded brands find themselves at a crossroads. The rules have changed.

So what replaces the modern corporation as we know it? In the 2001 article "e-R&D—the net@work," it was proposed that the 'network' may evolve to be the successor to 'scale'—size without weight, critical mass without massive expense."[3] And a great many business school professors have predicted the emergence of this model. In reality, that future is now. In the new economy, the bureaucratic form is replaced by the *network* form in which companies orchestrate their businesses activities across global ecosystems of employees, customers, manufacturing partners, distributors, and innovation networks. Companies such as Li & Fung already use globalization, outsourcing, the Internet, and other advantages to drive unprecedented speed to market, economics, and business flexibility. Li & Fung is a shining example of an established business that reinvented itself to fully capitalize on the new economy with impressive results. They had few examples to follow. In this book, the Challenge Driven Enterprise provides that roadmap for driving the needed change and is implementable on a variety of scales. It suggests a new operating system for businesses that focuses on what creates value and packages the work required efficiently so that it can be imported or exported to where it is best performed. Moving from the bureaucratic to the network form for some companies requires significant change. For other companies, it will require the deconstruction and reconstruction of the entire enterprise.

CDE has the unique benefit of substantially enhancing the effectiveness and efficiency of business performance while enabling new levels of innovation. In other words, you *can* have it both ways. But how should the CEO think about the transformation necessary to adopt these principles? And is change on this scale even possible?

The next section begins by clarifying the most important tools at the CEOs disposal: business strategy, corporate culture, and the senior leadership team. These are exceedingly powerful tools that are necessary and quite sufficient for the capable chief executive to not only lead great institutions, but to transform them when change is required. The overall topic of leadership and role of the CEO and senior management team in driving transformation will be addressed in the closing chapter.

# The Challenge Driven Enterprise as Business Strategy

For so much management science, the diversity of approaches to corporate strategy is quite remarkable. Some businesses focus on their "hedgehog" concept, with full credit given to Jim Collins, who wrote the excellent book *Good to Great*. Some companies operate like investment firms constantly looking for which industries and markets will yield exemplary returns and where there are assets and capabilities that can give them an advantage. Many employ a Michael Porter approach, who literally wrote the book *Competitive Strategy*, which applies a number of lenses to the strategy process. Very often the business strategy itself is essentially outsourced to management consultants. All of these approaches and others can deliver successful results when applied with rigor and vision. The problem is that good strategy work is hard, and most companies do a poor job of it.

Too many organizations apply corporate strategy in name only, choosing instead to do a form of corporate planning instead. Corporate planning focuses on headcount, cost management, and growth rates, and as a consequence most strategies are incremental. And generally, budgets are more closely pegged to financial performance and market conditions than where the next billion dollar opportunity is for investors. In other words, although you can strive to be strategic, to capitalize on market potential, to identify lucrative adjacencies, your strategy processes often produce incremental results at best.

These issues are particularly acute in large businesses, where developing strategy for a multibillion dollar corporation can be like plotting a course for a supertanker. The sheer scale and mass substantially limit the freedom to operate. For these organizations, managing risk to zero is the goal and therefore only incremental innovation is possible. Companies stick with what they know and can do with a high degree of confidence. So they plan and execute consistently and with precision, keeping pace and seldom deviating dramatically from the prior years' plans. All the while, they continue to invest, hire, and build bureaucracy as they always have. It should be no surprise that these organizations fail at creating disruptive innovation and find themselves increasingly challenged in their core markets by spirited lean agile competition. This isn't to say that all larger companies are inefficient or unable to drive radicle innovation: Apple, Amazon, and Google, for example, consistently outmaneuver the competition. Overwhelmingly though, it is clear that our businesses are held back by the sheer weight of the institutions we've created. Sadly, incrementalism and bloat are the silent killers of our businesses.

Small and midsize enterprises may have an advantage relative to larger organizations as less infrastructure and bureaucracy may mean more flexibility to execute and deliver on innovative strategies. This presents an intriguing opportunity to evolve into network models and adopters of CDE more fluidly than their larger counterparts. That said, smaller organizations often emulate the behaviors of the larger companies they aspire to become. All enterprises then, large and small, must re-imagine themselves.

Interestingly, with all the tools at their disposal to drive innovative strategies, it is remarkable how many organizations choose to create a new division or even a separate company to tackle entirely new business opportunities (for example, GM and Saturn). The rationale is that new ideas or the need for agile operations will be stifled by the organization. One wonders how many excellent business strategies are never executed because companies recognize the likelihood of failure within their own four walls. CEOs are externalizing the execution in these cases, which is good for business, but for the wrong reasons. If the organization and culture are toxic to new ideas or agile execution, how can it compete in the twenty-first century? The elephant in the room is that leadership, strategy, people, and corporate culture may all need to be remade to remain viable and competitive.

Let's now return to P&G, the subject of last chapter's case study. The Connect + Develop initiative emerged in response to the recognition that the well-known consumer products company would need to create new business on the order of $4 billion a year to maintain their shareholder commitments. CEO A.G. Lafley recognized that this kind of sustained growth could be accomplished only by engaging a whole world of potential innovation to drive new products and lines of business. Accordingly, he bet heavily on new partnerships, technology scouting, and innovation marketplaces such as InnoCentive. This permeated throughout the P&G organization, culminating in the development of a core capability that today accelerates access to new technologies, identifies new business opportunities, and helps to ensure P&G's dominance in the categories in which they compete. P&G recognized the power of this approach, particularly with respect to innovation, as a core element of their strategy and a vital source of competitive advantage. Today Connect + Develop and "Open Innovation" have become part of the P&G brand itself.

You must recognize that the Challenge Driven Enterprise is a foundational business strategy with broad reaching implications and one for which the Board of Directors and CEO must be deeply committed. The impact will cascade across the organization. In this brave new world, your organization is not limited by what skills and capabilities exist internally because they are available universally and on-demand. Factory construction lead-times are no longer impediments because manufacturing capacity is also available on-demand. Millions of innovators stand ready to design your products. Call centers and distribution hubs can be rented and are often better managed than owned facilities. You will focus most of your energy as a leader on the business opportunity and the application of capital that drives the best returns.

In the network form, strategy and the ability to orchestrate networks are the only core competencies that truly matter. And Challenges are both the building blocks and the glue that articulates, organizes, directs, tracks, and distributes resources and efforts efficiently. Business leaders may now focus their energies on the art of the possible. In this world, effectively managing complex ecosystems to leverage capital is the business competency that wins in the marketplace. Developing core and universal capabilities in creating new ideas, problem solving, communication, collaboration, and solution integration will become mission-critical as every opportunity is a challenge waiting to be solved. Finance managers, business development, program managers, and alliances all play elevated roles. This approach challenges major assumptions underlying existing business designs, including how you think about human capital, what assets do you own, and how much work can be externalized. In other words, this approach can dramatically impact underlying structure, headcount, and the balance sheet and, depending on the organization, the impact could be considerable. You will need to be intellectually honest by acknowledging most areas of the company are bloated and must become leaner and more agile. The temptation will be to take a traditional change management approach and to phase in elements and principles over time so as not to undermine the existing order, essentially the path of least resistance and the most likely to fail. Leaders must resist the temptation, making CDE a foundational strategy of the highest order and utmost urgency for the organization. And it may be the most significant impact this generation of business leaders will have on their organizations and the future.

# Remaking a Culture

How important a factor is culture when it comes to implementing a new strategy? A client of InnoCentive's who was reviewing an open innovation deployment plan for his organization said something so clear, succinct, and insightful that it stuck in our minds and we've never forgotten it. He said simply "Nice strategy. But in our business, culture eats strategy for lunch." And he was right. Transforming an organization, particularly one that is largely comfortable with the status quo, represents an enormous undertaking and one we examine in more detail.

Wikipedia has the following to say about culture in general:[4]

> In the twentieth century, "culture" emerged as a concept central to anthropology, encompassing all human phenomena that are not purely results of human genetics. Specifically, the term "culture" in American anthropology had two meanings: (1) the evolved human capacity to classify and represent experiences with symbols, and to act imaginatively and creatively; and (2) the distinct ways that people living in different parts of the world classified and represented their experiences, and acted creatively.

Although a bit abstract, the definitions applied to business are relevant. Corporate culture is the shared experiences and identity of the organization, and it is the foundation for expression and creativity. It is particularly interesting that leadership assumes you can make culture as easily as you define business strategy.

It is common today, even trendy, to talk about corporate culture and its importance to the success of organizations. We want to create winning cultures. We survey our staff and invest heavily in culture initiatives. Most will not admit to how little success senior leaders have had in harnessing culture effectively to create real business value much less changing or molding the culture.

## Change Is Difficult

To be clear, culture can be made and engineered; however, the longer a culture has been in existence and the larger the organization, the greater its mass and inertia and the more difficult it is to transform. Great force must be applied to have significant impact on existing and entrenched culture. A large application of force may be applied or many smaller repetitions like small pushes of a child's swing summing up to a large force over time. The former may be a CEO mandate, while examples of the latter may include training programs and employee culture initiatives. In actuality, both forms of force must be applied to really move culture, starting with the CEO. It is essential that each push on the organization is coordinated and drives employees in the same direction, making timing vital, just like pushes on a swing. The brutal reality is that most change initiatives will fail, not due to lack of resources, but due to lack of commitment, execution, and focus by the CEO and senior team.

As our organizations grew, significant bureaucracy developed to manage the complexity and scale of the business. Corporate culture impacts and is impacted by engagement at the top, middle, and bottom of the pyramid. Interestingly, the top may choose or even dictate a corporate culture, and the bottom may be more than willing to change and adopt with passion and conviction, but the midsection of the pyramid is the fundamental operating apparatus of the modern corporation. Mid-level management sets direction, compensation, and incentives, and has authority over the lion's share of what happens in enterprises. Generally, these managers have created a status quo to their liking and may well prefer the status quo to the unknown. This helps explain why culture is so difficult to change in large businesses. Organizations instinctively resist change and mid-level management arguably has the most to lose.

### Real Change Is Possible When Managed from the Top

When President Obama announced his open government initiative in 2010 as a follow-up to earlier campaign promises, many were surprised. He issued a presidential directive to all agencies in his control requiring them to submit detailed plans for opening up their processes and engaging U.S. citizens through use of technology and other means. He sent a clear signal and established the apparatus to ensure engagement by agency heads and administrators. Although still early, it is clear that U.S. government is moving toward the open model. W. Edwards Deming, famous for his approaches to quality and manufacturing, once said "You can expect what you inspect." The message here is simple: Culture can be your greatest ally but is also the greatest threat to any change. Executive-level leadership is required, as is constant focus and attention to reinforcing the message, and a clear understanding and articulation of the stakes. P&G recognized it could not continue to grow without dramatic change. President Obama recognized the potential to reinvent areas of government to be more efficient, effective, and democratic (the case study subject in Chapter 9, "Leadership").

Now we have said two things that may appear to be in conflict: first that organizations can drive their culture; and second, that corporate culture and mid-level management are enormously effective at resisting change, dooming most change management efforts to failure. But no contradiction exists. The reconciliation of the two realities is centered on the need for corporate change to be managed as a core strategy with CEO-level support and focus as well as actively managed and orchestrated programs to drive adoption, measure progress, and overcome barriers.

### *Empowerment and Communications*

General George Patton once said, "Never tell people how to do things. Tell them what to do and they will surprise you with their ingenuity." This is a powerful lesson that many leaders know well. The CEOs must paint the vision, establish the incentives, unleash the organization to deliver on the mission, and hold everyone accountable. And then they must breathe life into the vision every day at every opportunity.

Personnel issues can be the most difficult for any leader in any organization. Get it right, and almost anything is possible. Poor leadership and failing to deal with the people issues has been the downfall of many a strategic initiative. Although the CEOs must be the visionaries, champions, and the inspiration for change, they must also bear the ultimate accountability and responsibility for the inevitable people implications. Being direct, honest, and purposeful in an open and communicative way can ease the tension of the organization. But make no mistake, some of these actions will be difficult.

Jim Collins, Stanford University academic and author of a number of highly influential business books, emphasizes that there are two kinds of employees: those whom you want on the bus and those you don't. When the CEO of Procter & Gamble signaled in clear terms that change was coming in the organization and the need to be on the bus, he made it clear that some may not like where the bus is going. A CEO-led initiative to fundamentally transform a company in many cases requires a recasting of the leadership team and substantial adjustments in mid-level management. The uncomfortable reality is that many will need to exit the bus. The gentle pushing of the swing may simply not be enough and, for many organizations, may simply take too long. As business leaders, you are expected to make tough decisions and tradeoffs.

# Talent Management 2.0

Talent management in a global and connected world is a rich topic requiring real vision and a global perspective. Understanding the impact of deploying CDE to sales, customer service, manufacturing, finance, and all areas of the organization requires business savvy, a thorough understanding of business economics, a relentless commitment to organizational excellence, and a firm hand. In the CDE, the consuming focus is on identifying the problems whose solutions advance the overall strategy and drive shareholder gains. Everything else is secondary. We must resource and connect the organization with people and capabilities to bring life to this approach. The HR function has been about managing employees, but will refocus now in ways they have not in past. It becomes the strategic owner of key elements of CDE and the tools needed to give the organization the best access to the talent in order to deliver against the goals of the corporation. This is a fundamental elevation of the role of HR in most organizations, and one for which the leadership in those roles today will often fall short.

Some organizations, if they have not already, may establish the office of Chief Talent Officer, whose responsibility is to ensure recruitment and identification, development and enrollment, and retention and engagement of all talent, inside and outside the organization. And to use those tools to maximize company performance with a particular focus on maximizing shareholder value. Organizations will seek to fill this role with a visionary business executive who will be charged with operationalizing CDE in true partnership with the CEO. In the New World, these executives will likely be among the most influential and capable executives in the organization and among the potential succession pool for future CEOs.

## The Changing Nature of Work

The nature of work as you know it is changing rapidly. And labor markets are quickly moving to a freelancer economy, or a *Free Agent Nation*[5] as described by Daniel Pink in his excellent book by the same name. While businesses today are suffering a recession worse than any in recent memory, and while U.S. unemployment rate has exceeded 10 percent, nearly 3 million jobs remain unfilled. Businesses are chronically unable to staff key positions, particularly in areas in science, technology, engineering, and math. The reality is that the best talent is more empowered than ever, emboldened by technology and the ability to work where and how they choose. So, businesses must not only organize themselves more efficiently to remain competitive, but must also compete for the best talent. And increasingly, that talent is not interested in becoming a full-time employee of yours or any company. To make matters worse, the current generation entering the workforce, the millennial generation, shares that same view of employment. They will have on average eight jobs in their professional careers. They don't dislike the idea of full-time or lifelong employment, they simply choose to work when and how they want in an economy that gives them that the flexibility for the first time in history.

The changing nature of work will put additional stress on organizations designed to be operated as large monolithic institutions because these organizations have little experience managing talent outside of their employee base. The chief talent officer must think of real and virtual talent like a strategic supply chain. For example, consider Ford Motor Company that manages steel as a vital and scarce raw material whose availability and acquisition cost it cannot control. Because steel is its lifeblood, it applies sophisticated tools and methods as it actively manages its raw material supply chain. So the chief talent officer has two interrelated calls to action: He must drive the organization to an increasingly flexible and variable work model, while cultivating access to global talent, recognizing that any disruption in the supply line could wreak havoc on the business. Accessing the Long Tail discussed in Chapter 4, "The Long Tail of Expertise," becomes a critical success factor for the business. This reinforces the strategic role of the chief talent officer as a vital player in enabling the Challenge Driven Enterprise.

# The Role of Senior Leadership Is to Lead

Do not confuse commitment to effective people strategy, with commitment to every team member in the organization. The CEOs obligation is to the shareholders. As discussed, it is all too easy to ignore the long run in favor of the short run, namely protecting existing structures, people, and the status quo. Real change requires that some decisions will be unpopular. This is also why the CEO and the Board of Directors must be unified in adopting CDE principles.

Leadership may change, other core strategies may change, and the organization may look very different. Virtualizing more and more of the enterprise will create agile, lean, and more dynamic organizations, boosting competitiveness and improving profits. Make no mistake; this will not be easy and will be unpopular to many.

> In a survey of senior executives conducted recently by the Economist Intelligence Unit titled Global Firms in 2020,[6] a number of results were quite striking. Respondents said that in the next ten years:
>
> - 47% of respondents said the proportion of part-time workers would grow
> - 50% said their organizations would be flatter than in the past
> - 62% indicated there would be less job security
>
> When asked which skills will be the most important to your organization's success, the highest-rated were problem-solving skills at 42% and project management skills at 38%. Function- specific skills (for example, design and research) rated only 23%, near the bottom of the list.

And this is only the tip of the iceberg. There is no question that, intellectually, leadership teams know what their businesses must do to remain competitive. Now is the time to act.

The scale and magnitude of change needed for organizations intent on adopting this transformational approach need not consume senior leadership. And micromanaging change does not institutionalize it and too often ensures its failure. Becoming a CDE does require strong leadership. And traditionally, big projects require enormous overhead. So the conclusion, too easily made, is that the CDE requires a heavy hand and an enormous resource base dedicated to ensuring its success. Again, we assume that bureaucratic approaches are always the solution to minimizing risk of failure. There is no question that the whole of the enterprise will be impacted, but building a bureaucracy to eliminate a bureaucracy is not the answer.

The leader's role is to set the direction of the organization while enabling the culture and leadership to execute on the vision. The right approach here is not to manage this transformation like implementing an Enterprise Resource Planning system (for example, SAP or Oracle). Rather, it is to energize and inspire change across the organization. President Obama did not develop plans for each of the agencies. He set the strategic direction, instructed government officials to remove barriers to implementation, and demanded plans from each of the agency administrators. The White House involved the private sector in learning sessions with government officials to ensure knowledge transfer to accelerate adoption. And at every turn, administrators and staff were constantly reminded that the President was personally invested in making this initiative successful. This is a powerful template for engagement. Lead and empower and, as General Patton said, they will surprise you with their ingenuity.

## The CEO Conundrum

Growing great companies, delivering exceptional products and services, and creating wealth and value for shareholders are the charge of senior leadership. The essential truth is that maximizing shareholder returns over the long run is the singular goal that should matter most to the CEO and Board of Directors at the end of the day. Ironically, ensuring the best outcome in the long term and short term can be very much at odds, particularly with executive performance tied so closely to near-term company performance. It should be no surprise that thinking is so short term at most companies. And heavy use of equity and options does not eliminate the conflict. The reality is that optimizing company strategies for the short term often pushes company and CEO risk well into the future (and often to successors), while optimizing for the long term often pulls company and CEO risk into the present. Add to that the short average tenure of CEOs, and you realize the depth of moral hazard at play.

The CEO conundrum is this: Senior leaders and Boards of Directors are the stewards charged with maximizing shareholder returns over the long run. Yet when faced with making strategic decisions, their safe choice is too often the short-term view. Often it is only when their company is at the precipice, fighting for its survival, that the leadership is truly incented to make long-term decisions, and by this time it's often too late.

This conundrum is particularly acute in industries like pharmaceuticals and automotive where planning and capital commitments may span decades. When average CEO tenures are shorter than planning horizons, what is the incentive for leadership in these industries to champion significant evolution in the design and structure of their organizations (such as fundamentally changing the ratio of fixed to variable labor or choosing *not* to invest in another factory)? CEOs agonize over such decisions, and for the vast majority, implementing fundamental change is seldom contemplated seriously. Tragically, the U.S. automotive industry had to be on the brink of extinction to drive any real change.

As twenty-first–century competitive pressures mount, too few companies recognize how quickly they are approaching the precipice and that their own businesses designs (yes, the ones that served them so well in the twentieth century) will be the means of their own destruction. At precisely the time these companies need to be investing in the future and remaking themselves to compete effectively, their leadership is falling short, failing to make the tough decisions. CEOs must recognize that their companies already are or may soon be fighting for their very survival and that the best long-term strategy is a short-term imperative to reinvent themselves to be lean, virtual, open, and innovative. Leaders that fail to act are putting their businesses at great risk. Conversely, those leaders who act soon enough may create tremendous opportunity to lap the competition and to dominate their spaces well into the future.

The CDE will provide a roadmap for engaging in this journey to remake the organization, and leadership will require every tool in their arsenal.

## Make This Your Mission

As mentioned and reinforced throughout this book, the CEO's role is to build a great company to deliver excellent products and services that meet the needs of customers, and most important, to deliver outstanding returns to the shareholders. We live in a dynamic global economy where products are delivered at a breakneck pace, where new business ideas can go from concept to scale overnight, and where shocks to the economy can result in the destruction of companies previously thought too big to fail. Competition is fierce. Companies' designs are rooted in the bureaucratic form that emphasizes scale over flexibility. However leadership has an obligation to look out 10, 20, even 30 years. And in too many companies and industries, the easy decision continues to win out over the right decision. However, businesses are at a breaking point as the business landscape is evolving quickly and is unforgiving. The spoils go to the winner. Businesses and their leadership teams must now act.

CEOs have a unique opportunity to set their companies on a new path. CDE is a transformative vision of how innovative companies should operate in the twenty-first century, in a world that is global, networked, and fast-paced. Lou Gerstner reinvented IBM. A.G. Lafley set Procter & Gamble on a new course.

The contrarians will argue that shareholders have set the focus on quarterly earnings and performance in a way that discourages any form of risk-taking. They will argue that some changes are too big, and the company success in the past is the best predictor of success in the future. They will argue that no organization, its CEO, or Board of

Directors would rationally consider a transformation of this magnitude, unless collapse was imminent. It would be naïve to assume this course would be easy; however, most shareholders will buy into a vision and allow CEOs and leadership teams the latitude to execute on bold visions to create value. It's the lack of vision and forward thinking from the CEO and Board of Directors that is lacking, not the appetite to invest in the future. As we've said, the Challenge Driven Enterprise is a long-term strategy and vision. It is a transformation disguised as a program. And it is a unique opportunity for business leaders to leave a truly lasting legacy.

The next chapter provides a "playbook" for initiating the Challenge Driven Enterprise in your organization that we hope will provide not only a general set of tools as well as a common language, but also the basis on which begin to put thoughts into action immediately.

# Case Study: Virtual Software Development: How TopCoder Is Rewriting the Code

As quoted in this chapter, General George Patton said, "Never tell people how to do things. Tell them what to do and they will surprise you with their ingenuity." TopCoder, a $20 million software developer, has done just that, using a challenge-driven approach to deliver code faster, cheaper and, most of all, better than traditionally organized companies can on their own. A testament to TopCoder's quality is that organizations such as Eli Lilly and NASA have hired TopCoder for their projects.[7]

Here's how TopCoder does it: TopCoder has nurtured a community of more than 250,000 software developers who provide the basis of TopCoder's on-demand "workforce." These coders are not TopCoder employees, and they don't work on salary. Instead, TopCoder organizes the coding work into challenges, each with a specific end goal. TopCoder announces the challenge, the goal, and the winning prize money that will be awarded to the top two solutions. The solutions are evaluated by a panel from the community. Usually, the contributed code is tested by the community in a separate challenge, with winners in that challenge being rewarded for "breaking" the code.

Programmers can enter any challenge they chose and deliver their code. So who would want to do coding for free, on the chance of being one of the two prize winners? The answer, simply put, is "the best coders." TopCoder founder Jack Hughes is a coder himself, and he knows what motivates software developers. "I started as a programmer," he says, "and I knew that good developers love to compete and compare and learn from each other."[8] Only the top two winners get prize money, but every contributor gets feedback on their code[9] and TopCoder tracks and posts a host of metrics on each member, including contests entered, quality, reliability, and amount won. The best coders love coding—it's their hobby and passion, not just a profession. "They work partly for fun, and for their professional and social networks," Hughes said.[10] In short, developers love to show their peers how smart they are and compete with each other to develop the best software code.

Besides peer motivation, the prize money (often tens of thousands of dollars) is set by the market as well. If TopCoder isn't getting as much participation in a challenge as it wants, it increases the prize money.

TopCoder also excels at setting the specifications for each challenge, namely breaking the task down into a series of discrete components that are easily communicated and can be assembled together. Getting the modularity right is essential so that programmers can participate in the challenges during their spare time. Good programmers are in short supply, and of the 250,000-strong TopCoder community, 5 percent to 10 percent participate regularly. "We provide an on-demand, variable workforce," Hughes says. "These are people who have excess capacity, are between jobs, or want intellectual stimulation. Their incentive can be financial, community, or recognition."[11] The challenges have specific start and stop dates, although the time that a developer spends on the task is never tracked. "We don't care about that," Hughes says, "the focus is on quality."[12]

Orchestration of the work remains an important TopCoder function. Complex software code must be broken down into manageable modules and coordinated. As Jeff Howe, author of *Crowdsourcing* and credited with popularizing the term, said, "Someone needs to be calling the shots saying 'OK you guys work on this, OK now there's a new contest and it's to test this winning code to see who can break this winning code'—someone needs to be setting these sorts of tasks. It's not so much that the crowd can't perform complex tasks, but it is the case that someone needs to be running the show; someone needs to be breaking down the problem."[13]

TopCoder has attracted top programmers to its community. Naturally, other companies have eyed the community as a source for their own new hires. Pharmaceutical giant Eli Lilly was one of those firms. But the power of the TopCoder model is the diversity and flexibility of its workforce, not just one or two members. "We realize that [TopCoder] is truly a network of top programmers and also a very scalable way of delivering solutions where we don't have to own every piece of the puzzle. We can still leverage all the expertise for just the pieces that we need," said Everett Lee, manager of discovery research IT at Lilly.[14] Lilly realized it was easier to tap the network, especially for large projects, than to try to create the network by hiring parts of it for its own staff. In addition, TopCoder spent three years at the outset developing and nurturing the community before it used the community for any client work. "They spent years and they served the community first." Howe said. "What will the community think is fun? What do our people like to do? Our people like to compete. Our people like to see who's the best coder. They like to play games with each other," Howe said.[15] TopCoder succeeded by investing the time to understand and nurture the community.

Transparency is another critical success factor. "Volunteers will not accept secrecy, game-playing and favoritism," write Julian Birkinshaw and Stuart Cainer in their study of TopCoder for MLab. "So TopCoder plays it straight: The amount of prize money, and the rules of the game, are defined upfront. During competitions, if one developer asks a question, all of the developers see the answer. Peer review, rather than the judgment of TopCoder's executives, is the basis for any subjective evaluations that are made in the competitions."[16]

In the end, TopCoder's on-demand workforce model gives it access to the best talent combined with a flexible cost base. The orchestration of the work includes building a library of "reusable Java and .Net components that it uses to supplement developer efforts. Its members compete to produce the best code for the catalog, and winners continue to get paid royalties every time the code is reused."[17] The transparency sustains trust. The result is that TopCoder claims that it can produce applications in 100 fewer days than industry norms, at half the cost, and at least twice the quality (based on the 'constructive cost model' aka COCOMO, a common software-development benchmark)."[18]

In true network design fashion, Hughes said that from the beginning he knew he wanted to approach software creation as a discipline. "The key to quality," Hughes says, "is to avoid monolithic systems in favor of component-based systems."[19]

# 8

## The Challenge Driven Enterprise Playbook

"The price of success is hard work, dedication to the job at hand, and the determination that whether we win or lose, we have applied the best of ourselves to the task at hand."

—*Vince Lombardi*

## Overview

Part I, "Challenge Driven Innovation," discussed the inherent limitations of traditional innovation models and then provided a theoretical and applied framework for firms to substantially improve their innovation effectiveness going forward. The work of well-known business leaders and world-class academics, the authors' observations from years of business experience with both unwieldy bureaucracies and with emerging open innovation marketplaces, including Inno-Centive, meaningfully informed the practical approaches promoted. Chapter 6, "The Challenge Driven Enterprise," and Chapter 7, "Transformation," introduced CDE and discussed at length the issues and stakes to be considered by the CEO and Board of Directors as they contemplate transformational change. This chapter provides a general and actionable framework for planning and initiating the requisite corporate transformation. In addition, a number of techniques and considerations based upon years of field experience are identified.

# The Playbook

In football, the playbook is essential, enabling the orchestration of many players in highly dynamic game situations. Its actual utility is in its simplicity, economy, and modular form. By predefining both general and special purpose plays, the coach can direct the team to execute against most any strategy in a highly efficient and coordinated fashion. And importantly, the coach can flexibly adjust the plays to react to emerging challenges and opportunities on the field. The goal in assembling The CDE Playbook is to provide a similar toolset for implementing the Challenge Driven Enterprise that leaders can adapt and apply as needed. The playbook is intended to be reasonably comprehensive and may be used as the basis of an overall plan for the enterprise. It is important, though, to recognize that every organization is different and that significant judgment should be applied. Assume that you as the coach must choose the plays from the book that make sense in your organization.

The analogy of football is actually a powerful one. While the focus in this chapter is the playbook, it should not be lost on the reader that every game has an uncertain outcome. Winning is a function of the strategy of game play, resilience and talent of the players, preparedness, and esprit de corps of the team—indeed, many factors, obvious and subtle. Great coaches consider every dimension and strive to leave little to chance. Now the rules of the game are changing and the coach must rethink everything. But there is one constant; it is still about winning. And great coaches know how to adapt and win.

The CDE Playbook is organized into seven sections that are broadly applicable and logically sequenced, recognizing that a number of these activities will be going on in parallel and that different parts of the organization may be executing against the playbook at various speeds and on different timelines. For example, some organizations will run pilot activities while they build the business case and secure "buy in" and approval from senior leadership, while others will take a top down enterprise-wide approach from the onset.

### Challenge Driven Enterprise Playbook

    I.   Board of Directors and C-Level Commitment

    II.   Promote Early Trial and Adoption

    III.   Virtualize the Business Strategy

    IV.   Establish the CEO Mandate

    V.   Create and Empower CDE Task Force

    VI.   Align and "Ready" the Organization

    VII.   Select Enablers and Enroll Partners

Generally, the CEO and senior leadership roles are the focus in this chapter because it simplifies the discussion. However, there will clearly be cases in which senior managers, directors of the company, and others will drive the transformational change. It is understood that these concepts will be adapted as needed. Further, organizations should not hesitate to scale down the approach to divisions or departments, providing they recognize that a CEO sponsored transformational agenda is the ideal approach recommended by the authors. Use of the playbook is equally valid in other sectors, such as government, education, and even the Not-for-Profit (NFP) world. Finally, we provide guidance and ideas at the end of the chapter on translating the playbook to various applications.

# I. Board of Directors and C-Level Commitment

Not surprisingly, this first section of The CDE Playbook may well be the most important. The resolve and determination needed to successfully evolve the organization is considerable and not without risks. CEOs and Boards of Directors must commit in no uncertain terms and see it through to the end. But, before the CEO pronouncements are published in *The Wall Street Journal* and questions are answered on quarterly investor calls, the Board of Directors and CEO must intensely consider the Challenge Driven Enterprise and all the implications. The actual decision to be made is whether to substantially reengineer the enterprise, adopting CDE as the framework on which the business will operate, well into the future.

### Planning, Budgeting, Measuring, and Self-Funding

Resources, including capital and personnel, must be allocated and available for the transformational efforts needed to be successful. Planning and budgeting are significant considerations, yet we can provide only guidance here in terms of broad generalities. Certain activities can be managed for modest investments of resources and money—for example, pilots and strategic planning. At the other end of the spectrum, "reengineering the enterprise" is a substantial undertaking and will involve considerable efforts and costs. Finance will "own" the multiyear plan to manage the economics and metrics: modeling benefits and costs, building the budgets, ensuring accountability and transparency, and instilling a measurement rigor into the organization. It also means finance will have a crucial role in the deployment of CDE, tracking progress, and reporting on gains to leadership and to Wall Street. It is worth noting that as mentioned in earlier chapters, many organizations have chosen metrics that actual perpetuate the current systems, rewarding the wrong behavior. A critical analysis of the measures appropriate for the company going forward is important in driving the needed change.

Dividends will begin to accrue surprisingly early in the transformation that can be directed toward later phases of the program. This represents a significant opportunity from a financial perspective, but also for corporate messaging. Gains from early investments will be reinvested and largely fund ongoing implementation as the company continually improves its competitiveness—a powerful message. We recommend building your plan and setting financial assumptions such that the transformation is entirely self-funding and potentially profitable in 3 to 5 years.

For some organizations, this is not only a significant investment in the future of the company, but it may also qualify as restructuring. And as such, there may be opportunities to apply beneficial accounting treatments to related expenses and, in some cases, you may quality for R&D credits or other inducements. You should use experts in financial accounting, taxation, financing, and other areas to uncover all the opportunities. The financial implications are significant and the technical expertise of the finance team will be tested, so the CFO should plan accordingly.

Rationalizing the organization, particularly in the context of this approach, creates another opportunity: Programs that run counter to the long-term objectives of the program should be considered for reductions or eliminated altogether, further freeing up capital to support the program. Why build a new factory when you will likely use contract manufacturing capacity available in Asia or elsewhere? Strategy and Finance should take the point on assessing the current portfolio of major projects to identify candidate expenditures that can be better applied, completely consistent with the principles of CDE. Consider viewing this exercise as its own Challenge: Which programs may be scaled back or canceled to generate $20MM annually, which can be applied to the CEOs mandate?

There is significant time and work in planning such an undertaking. Some organizations may begin with early trials and others will aggressively move right to full-blown reengineering efforts. The choice depends upon the corporate culture, resources, and the CEOs confidence in the organization's capability to change.

Finally, organizations are exceedingly adept at judging the CEO and their level of commitment by how they allocate resources and their management attention. At the risk of hyperbole, bold means bold. Any less and the organization will discount the change from the onset and seriously handicap the likelihood of success.

## Commitment

Enrolling the board, investors, employees, partners, and other stakeholders is vital. The CEO must enroll and engage all his constituents and bring them along as partners in the journey ahead. The Board must be sold on the long-term benefits, the risk reward tradeoffs, and the time table to deliver on the vision. Employee engagement is vital to the success of the initiative, requiring a significant and ongoing enrollment and communications strategy. Investors must understand how the economics of the business will change, expected short- and long-term implications to share price and dividends and other structural implications to the company's financials. Partners must understand that the company will be going through a transformation, and for some partners, this will create opportunity. And there will be other stakeholders as well, running the gamut from the banks to the analyst community. The CEO must anticipate the reactions of all these entities and have a plan to enroll them as partners.

The potential conflicts that exist with CEOs, senior executives, and corporate boards making major commitments with long-term implications have already been discussed (the CEO Conundrum from Chapter 7). Leaders seek to capture upside while steering away from risk and instinctively avoid engaging in programs they believe could fail big, particularly when the benefits may be years away. And as a general rule, this strategy serves executives well. Unfortunately, this risk aversion can also lead to catastrophic failures (for example, the U.S. auto industry). Even when the future viability and competitiveness of a company or industry is clearly in question, executives often cannot bring themselves to make the really tough structural choices. Too often it takes a crisis to bring leaders and organizations to commit to change, as demonstrated during the recent recession. CDE represents an opportunity to remake the organization in the face of increasing competition, substituting an aging model for a new more agile, innovative, and efficient one. Organizations with real vision and courage opt for change well before staring into abyss. Some may never make the commitment. But for those that do, it is important that they fully comprehend the consequences—a significant reengineering of the enterprise which means rewriting the strategy, reallocating resources, and focusing significant leadership attention toward bringing the CDE to life for the organization. They must commit fully to the vision. After the decision is made and ratified by the Board, it is time to act.

# II. Promote Early Trial and Adoption

In any case, promoting pilots to demonstrate the potential for "open" and "networked" concepts to change the rules is a good strategy. This section discusses using trials most effectively to secure early learnings, create internal wins, and support adoption.

Creating early wins and success stories can capture the imagination of the organization and provide tremendous opportunities to apply the basic concepts and to learn from early trial. Coupled with the clear message from the top of the organization that change is coming, leadership and staff can see the opportunity not only to get on the bus, but also to help drive.

### *Utilize Challenges Strategically and Organize Events Around Them*

You need to teach the organization about the concepts, while establishing the foundation on which broader programs and efforts will be built. Organizing challenge events for maximum effect can be incredibly effective at this stage. For example, enrolling the entire organization in identifying new product ideas or focusing an R&D group on proving out open innovation on an important high-profile project is both empowering for staff and will also create an excitement and buzz. Business development can be tasked to identify the potential partnerships to accelerate product innovation. There is no limit to the number or variety of events that could be constructed to illustrate and highlight the concepts behind CDE. However, focusing on a few events with broad visibility and high volume potential may have maximum effect. These pilots need strong leadership and sufficient resources to ensure success.

InnoCentive frequently designs programs for corporations. Figure 8.1 outlines a typical pilot structure for early stage Open Innovation adopters.

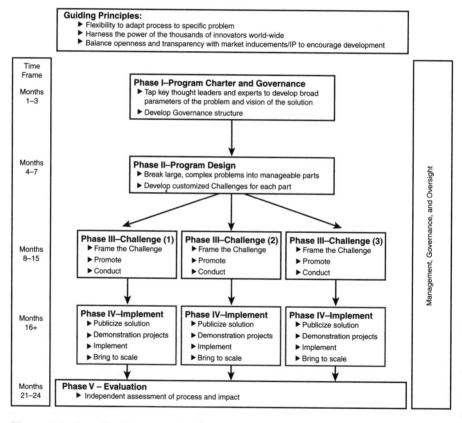

**Figure 8.1    InnoCentive sample pilot structure**

Source: InnoCentive

Further, this can be a crucible for understanding the scale of behavioral and cultural change needed in the months and years ahead and identifying gaps in capabilities and skill sets needed in the organization going forward. Thoughtful choices at this stage can have a big impact. But remember, the status quo will instinctively protect the status quo. If you want the organization to prove to itself the great potential inherent in breaking the mold, you need to give permission to employees in the organization, encourage them to take risks, and be vigilant in ensuring that bureaucracy and passive aggression does not impede employee's efforts. Hand-picking leaders and projects to ensure success at this stage may be necessary.

### *Evaluate Business Impact and Document Learnings*

Rigorously evaluate the pilot programs, translating the results into tangible business terms and impact. Properly designed, the measurements can have a strong economic basis and translate effectively to financial performance. CDE is about strategy and competitiveness. Resist the temptation to message the programs simply in terms of the numbers. Cost-savings, for example, is important and alone may justify the leadership focus, but it will not be sufficient to inspire the organization or to support the transformational vision. And it could actually work against the overall strategic message. In addition to the economics, relate the successes to advancing the mission in other tangible and intangible ways, for example, improving product time-to-market and beating out the competition or reducing manufacturing defects and thus improving customer satisfaction. Bringing a product to market in record time that was identified through partnership should be heralded as a coup for the company, and it signals that you don't need to invent it to profit from it. This can keep the message anchored in strategic terms, while ensuring the economic basis justifying the overall program is intact and beyond question.

After the results are in, success stories should be promoted across the organization to maximize effect.

### Promote the Successes

Successes are beachheads, early wins on which the larger programs will be built. They are the basis of many of the stories that will be told as the transformation builds. Promote not only the ideas, but also the divisions and departments that made them successful. Make heroes out of the leaders and practitioners. In doing so, you give further permission to think boldly in the organization. These are triumphs and are powerful portents of the change to come. Make these stories legendary.

# III. Virtualize the Business Strategy

At its heart, the CDE is an organization that has virtualized its business strategy and that expertly orchestrates the execution of its vision. It has transformed structurally and culturally to achieve its goals and to maximize shareholder returns. However, effectively translating those words into action requires more than just dedication and making assignments. It requires a compelling strategy with rigorous attention to detail and new structural, operational, and financial models of the business. Such an undertaking cannot be managed without risk. The prudent CEO invests heavily to ensure the strategy is comprehensive, risks are understood and minimized, and that progress can be metered and adjusted as the program progresses.

### Establish Guiding Principles

Guiding principles establish a basis of expectation and a benchmark against which important decisions can be made consistently across the organization. By weaving CDE concepts into the principles, the CEO effectively distributes his expectations and delegates responsibility for CDE at the same time. The CEO should communicate these guiding principles frequently to senior leadership and with staff wherever possible.

The following example illustrates the point:

**Sample Guiding Principles**

We will...

- Orchestrate value creation through partnering, markets, and ecosystems
- Externalize functions, projects, and work wherever possible
- Eliminate fixed cost and infrastructure; and maximize capital flexibility

In a nutshell, these principles state that in the twenty-first-century enterprise, value is created by *what* you do that is of value to your customer and nothing more. *How* you do it, from research to manufacturing are secondary. Winning companies will be masters at orchestrating the people and networks to capture that value. And by doing so, they will create shareholder value.

### Evolve the Business Strategy

This is an exercise not only on focusing on what's important, but also on converting the organization from its bloated and inflexible "bureaucratic" form to the virtual "network" form with all its inherent benefits. And it can be both clarifying and liberating. Be careful, if the effort to remake the strategy is not focused, it runs a real danger of collapsing under its own weight. P&G committed to enabling every aspect of open innovation in a company that had been closed and inward focused; it did not rethink whether to sell toothpaste or how big the consumer products market actually is.

**Ask provocative questions:**

- Could new business opportunities be exploited if we had more resources at our disposal? What could that mean to the future of the company?
- Could we substantially reduce time to market for new products and features if we engaged innovators around the world in product development and R&D processes?

- Is it possible to improve efficiency without reducing customer satisfaction by shifting customer service and other services to companies that specializes in those capabilities?

It is understood that none of these are purely financial decisions of course, but recognize that power of challenging the process to push the potential benefits to the limits. Every area of the business represents an opportunity for reengineering.

Consider using experienced practitioners or consultants to assist the organization in virtualizing the strategy for one simple reason: They have no pride of ownership in the existing strategy of the company. For some organizations, the optimal approach will be to allocate senior strategy resources and those of trusted advisors to develop the initial guiding principles and high-level planning to drive the more expensive effort of redesigning the company strategy at which time using more traditional internal and external consultants and partners may be appropriate. In any event, it is vital that the senior team "own" the process at all times.

### Model Long-Term Shareholder Value Implications

The strategy has been overhauled, early candidate projects identified, and the execution plans finalized, but it remains vital that all these efforts be tied to the long-term value of the company and directly to shareholder returns. It is understood that nothing is known with certainty; however, the financial rigor needed to operate in the CDE can be applied to the decision making even at this stage. For example, you can estimate the implications of the competition gaining five points of market share at your expense due to more inspired product innovation. The goal at this stage is not absolute precision. It is to objectively compare the organization as it exists today against the CDE vision and to translate the benefits for shareholders, analysts, employees, and other stakeholders.

Long-term shareholder value can be addressed qualitatively and quantitatively by focusing on the important strategic questions, thoughtfully valuing choices and options, and applying common sense thresholds to the analyses. Taken together, this can establish the case for virtualizing the business and do so in compelling terms. And in so doing, the CEO can create measurable and tangible goals for the organization. P&G calculated that it needed 50 percent of its innovation to come from the outside to continue to deliver on its growth in EPS commitments. And then it did exactly what it promised.

# IV. Establish the CEO Mandate

Successful CEOs focus the organization on a small number of key initiatives and some choose a single theme or strategy that defines their administration. The CDE can rise to that level, due to the strategic, structural, and competitive implications of its adoption. By making the CDE a mandate, everyone in the organization will understand the importance and commitment attached to this program by the CEO and the Board of Directors.

Jim Collins and Jerry Porras, in their book *Built to Last*, discussed the power of what they called Big Hairy Audacious Goals (or BHAGs) whose clarity and simplicity can drive impressive focus. They said "A true BHAG is clear and compelling, serves as unifying focal point of effort, and acts as a clear catalyst for team spirit. It has a clear finish line, so the organization can know when it has achieved the goal; people like to shoot for finish lines."[1] Examples of BHAGs potentially relevant to your organization could include commitments to"30% of innovation coming from the outside within 5 years" or "50% of the workforce being virtual or variable in 5–10 years."

The use of simple and clearly articulated goals has a secondary benefit: it challenges the organization to think differently and boldly and reinforces strategy at every sounding. HR will ask, "Should we be hiring that many people if our goal is the virtual organization?" And manufacturing may ask, "Can we outsource manufacturing instead of building the next factory?" Elevating the CDE to that of a core strategy ensures that the entire organization understands the CEOs resolve and commitment to its success. And therefore, the entire organization will "own" the strategy and feel it has permission to challenge the status quo.

In communications, it is imperative that organizations tie CDE to long-term shareholder objectives and other key strategies of the company—for example, the need to improve time-to-market for products, to maximize capital available for investment in the business, or to react quickly to changing business conditions. When understood, this approach yields singular objectives that can compel both the core strategy and its adoption.

### Enroll Senior Leadership

The senior leadership team must be unified in the vision and must charge forward to execute the strategy with all the zeal and passion of the CEO. This of course requires that they be fully enrolled as partners in the transformation. Their engagement is crucial and without their support, success will be elusive. The CEO should recognize that as the CDE principals are applied, the definition of senior management's respective departmental responsibilities could be altered substantially. And they will be keenly aware of the implications. Further, the makeup of the senior team itself could change. The best advice is to sell the senior team on the vision and involve them in key elements of the planning. Be open and honest in describing the future state and their role in it and the potential new opportunities that may emerge. Make every attempt to find these leaders appropriate seats on the bus, but don't be afraid to counsel out executives who will not or cannot adapt accordingly. The whole senior leadership needs to be on the bus or efforts will be compromised.

Clearly any transformation of this magnitude will have far reaching implications and the CEOs commitment to this initiative must acknowledge the need for substantial cultural change, only possible with the support of leadership. She must demand accountability and drive engagement using every tool at her disposal, including bonus programs, recognition programs, hiring, promotion, and firing (more on this later). These can be crucial to projecting and actualizing the mandate.

You must eliminate the 'More is better' management culture. Notions of bigger is better must be replaced with lean and mean. In fact less is more. As mentioned in the prior chapter, we've all been indoctrinated in the myth that bigger must be better in all things: headcount, budget, support staff, assets, and so on. This mentality must be broken, and the CEO has unique opportunity to reset these elements of culture, particularly management culture in the organization.

### *Communicate Clearly, Openly, and with Conviction*

The CEO and senior team must couple their efforts with clear and transparent communication to everyone involved. Consider the importance of the CEO speaking to the business as part of an effective program to drive irrevocable change into the organization. The CEOs voice will not only communicate the importance and commitment vital at this stage, it will also help manage the organization's natural anxiety that comes with any kind of change. This is not just an effort to reengineer the enterprise or to restructure spending; the CEO must convey a clear and unambiguous belief that this is vital to the future of the organization, and perhaps to the long-term viability of the company, and that new opportunity will emerge as a result. If the organization hears clear and transparent language coming in earnest from their CEO, it can understand the need for change and be open to it. The anxiety will never go away, but may be reduced, enabling the organization to focus on the future rather than dwelling on the present. Through use of this language, the CEO mandate becomes apparent. Reengineering the enterprise is a form of renewal. The reaction of many will be anxiety and fear; others will be intrigued and energized. Some will hear the opportunity of a lifetime knocking at their door.

So after the overall strategies have been articulated, business models updated, and the organization enrolled, it is now time to convert all the thinking, choices, models, and assumptions into a cogent multiyear plan for execution. Operationalizing it requires a dedicated and focused team, which is discussed next in Section V, "Create and Empower the CDE Task Force."

# V. Create and Empower the CDE Task Force

In the prior chapter, the argument was made that the effective CEO focuses on the strategy, culture, and senior leadership. She must enable the organization to change, not by micromanaging the details, but by empowering the organization and holding it accountable. In general terms, operationalizing the transformation requires installing a capable task force to oversee the details of implementation, recognizing that overcoming cultural and structural hurdles will require talented leadership and real perseverance. In a large organization, this task force can be expected to play an important role for 2 to 5 years depending on the degree of transformation required, the size of the organization, and the complexity of the business. This section discusses the key responsibilities of this team and its charter.

### Installation of the Overall Champion and Leader of the CDE Task Force

This initiative must have an overall operating champion with impeccable credibility and substantial leadership ability. This must be someone who can inspire the change needed while acting as a trusted agent of the CEO. Potential candidates will be many things, including a strategist, a tactician, a field marshal, and a politician, if they are to be successful. And the choice of this leader is one of the more important that the CEO will make with respect to bringing CDE to life in her organization.

We recommend that a senior leader be chosen and dedicated to this program, potentially someone who is prominent in the succession line to the chief executive position. And as such, this person will be fully capable to appreciate the far-reaching implications of her actions and the importance of her mission, while having a deep understanding of the current organization and the way things are done today. The Champion will report on progress to the CEO and to the Board of Directors as needed and should not be afraid of controversy or change.

### *Coordination of Strategy, Execution, and Progress Reporting*

The CDE task force will take primary responsibility for executing the vision, engaging the whole organization in culture change and change management activities, and measure and report back on progress to the CEO. In large organizations, the task force is a dedicated team that includes extended teams that reach across the business. Positioning is important and the task force must be viewed as an extension of the CEOs office with the entire mandate that entails.

The task force should be afforded significant authority, responsibility, and accountability. Although this initiative is a CEO-level mandate, the task force should manage the program and should only require intervention by the CEO around key strategic decisions and some early operational matters. Early in the process, the CEO may intercede more frequently, reinforcing the goals, expectations, and gravity of the mandate.

The CDE task force should be in constant communication with leadership in targeted areas of the business, requiring each of these areas to identify opportunities, operationalize plans, and to update the task force periodically on progress. The task force will be the air traffic control system for implementing the CDE and depending on the overall plan established by the organization, there may be a few or several departments, divisions, or functions at various stages of execution at any point in time.

Each targeted area of the business must provide a cogent plan that is realistic and aggressive, while balancing risk and long-term gain. In addition, these plans must be reconciled across the organization in time and space. Programs behind schedule or in need of attention will become apparent through this level of tracking. The task force will also have excellent visibility into key wins, emerging best practices, and where talented CDE capable leaders are developing.

As we have said before, the status quo is quite effective at maintaining itself. Experience teaches us that these exercises typically produce incrementalist plans at best in their first iterations. Reasons given will be "we cannot jeopardize the customer experience, can we?" or "we already employ the smartest people in our field!" or "now is not the best time to reorganize." These reactions should all be expected. They are natural, but what happens next is the most important. You must demand these teams, functions, and divisions to come back, again and again, until plans that comprehend and embrace the change needed are presented. This is an area where outside advisors or dedicated practitioners can play a vital role in challenging and supporting these efforts.

The CDE task force should apply good management oversight in addition to common sense to ensure that the various functions will effectively and efficiently transform the organization to the desired state while managing risk across the entire system. For example, the heavier use of outsourced providers should be balanced to give the organization sufficient power and influence to ensure quality and dependable service levels, particularly for critical functions. Choosing technologies and tools to enable the future state are also examples in which consolidated requirements across the teams and standardizing training and methods could provide substantial benefits.

### Identify and Prioritize Internal Opportunities for Reengineering

Not all the opportunities will be identical, and some will clearly drive more upside than others. Look for opportunities to have significant impact in the early years, big hitters, and low-hanging fruit. Leadership already has a good idea where to start. Why are you hiring 1,000 engineers? Should you be building call centers when India has excess capacity at a substantially lower cost base? Can you license the technology rather than buying the company? And by focusing on a few high-impact opportunities for reengineering, the likelihood of success increases as does the magnitude of the gains for the early wins.

Some organizations find that creating new structures are particularly effective when fresh ideas run the risk of being hamstrung by the existing culture or organization and in some cases go so far as to create entirely new companies. This can be a useful tactic, particularly suited in applications such as creating entirely new products or establishing new business lines, although its scalability for broad transformation is limited.

So whether identifying key functions, projects, or divisions, thoughtful selection of initial targets in the early years may prove far superior to tackling every aspect of the change at once. Likelihood of success will be higher, early dividends will be secured, success stories created, and risks minimized. But to be clear, this approach must be part of an overt, committed, comprehensive plan for change. Anything less may run the risk of undermining the transformation.

### Cross-Fertilize Opportunities

In this process, the CDE task force should look for every opportunity to use its coordination role to unlock upside for the company and shareholders. One manufacturing division may be developing capacity or capabilities unknown to another. Or R&D agendas could be advanced more efficiently if rationalized and executed through open innovation and partnership channels. In the strategy, planning, and ongoing execution phases of the project, the task force must maintain a deep understanding of the various touch points between efforts as well as overall opportunities to "connect the dots" wherever possible. Any opportunity to leverage learnings, methods, and resources should be exploited. Further, with critical focus, significant and surprising opportunities will be identified for synergy and elimination of waste.

### Regular Communications

Regular communications are critical in the tone, intensity, and excitement because they can improve execution efforts and constantly reinforce the central transformational theme across the organization.

You need a well-defined CDE scorecard for the whole company and periodic summary-level progress reports. They should have a fairly wide distribution published regularly on the intranet for access by the entire organization. Further by communicating and archiving best practices, success stories, tips and advice from the gurus, and so on, a new body of learning and methods emerges that will be invaluable. And integrating these communications efforts with broader internal and external corporate communications will further reinforce the message and the resolve to transform the company.

Finally, the CDE task force, while being held accountable by the CEO, must hold the entire organization accountable, not only to execute the CDE agenda, but also to deliver fundamental and durable change. The task force is the sharp point of the spear, and its efforts can make or break the overall initiative. While its authority comes from the CEO commitment whose constant support and visible attention is vital to the success of the transformation, it must own the transformation and provide its own strong leadership.

# VI. Align and "Ready" the Organization

The CDE requires a significant paradigm shift from that of most organizations today. Along with that shift comes the implication that most parts of the organization will undergo change, some more so than others. The prior section focused on establishing the CDE task force, an effort with a beginning, middle, and end. Now we consider opportunities to align and "ready" the entire organization for the transformation. Some of these activities belong to the CEO, some to the task force, and some to other areas of the organization. We will discuss management systems, reducing barriers to adoption, capabilities, key roles, and other considerations in this section.

## *Remake the Management Systems*

Our management systems define how the organization functions internally and with the rest of the world. These systems include structure and hierarchy, information flow and decision making, and process controls among others.

We must rethink these areas because they both enable and constrain organizational behavior. Want to change the behavior? Consider changing the systems. For example, the US military found that the new realities of warfare required more empowerment and agility in the field after generations of training soldiers to operate in highly structured command and control environments began to fail. It became clear after 2001 that the systems were no longer able to meet the challenges of modern warfare. Consequently, chain of command, training programs, recruitment, and rules of engagement have adapted considerably in support of the military's mission.

While each corporation's systems are unique, the basics structures are similar, largely because they are all based on the bureaucratic form (need to minimize transaction costs, etc). We mention two related areas as foundational alterations you should consider for remaking your management systems: functional decoupling and competition.

Most of your functions are tightly coupled. Consider how sales is related to marketing or products relationship with manufacturing. The old form required this linkage to maximize scale economies. In the new world, every business leader should be striving for efficiency and while marketing must "own" the message, sales is paying the bill, literally and figuratively. By adopting an outcome mentality, inside and out, each function will hold its own ecosystem more accountable than in the past, highlighting gaps and challenges, while suffering less the bureaucracy and inefficiency that many organizations have become accustomed. The second, but related, concept is competition. Here we go even further to say that product may call out manufacturing for not being cost effective for example. Controls must be in place, but if manufacturing cannot improve its operations and match external costs standards then there may be a business case for moving contracts outside. The controls must ensure that business objectives are met across the system, but we all know that a substantial share of inside work is inefficient and poorly managed. By redefining functional coupling and introducing competition, accountability, transparency, and efficiency are all brought front and center. And in the process, the organization will begins evolve itself toward the network form and will begin to exercise its new orchestration skillset in the process.

### Address Structural Barriers to Adoption

There are many structural barriers to adoption, some of which were discussed in prior chapters. The CDE task force, with timely engagement of the CEO, should be breaking down barriers as they emerge and identifying future roadblocks to adoption.

For example, the legal function is likely entrenched in protecting the organization, staff, and existing assets as it has done for years. Opening up processes, actively and aggressively in-licensing and out-licensing technology, using emerging talent networks, and partnering as a primary strategy are all examples of new behaviors and capabilities that will stress existing practices. HR is traditionally tasked with managing employees. As a consequence, developing robust and reliable talent pools of virtual workers will almost certainly fall outside its base of experience. The same realizations will be made whether looking at brand management, product development practices, financial accounting, and many other areas of the company. The point is that the CDE task force needs to play an aggressive leadership role in identifying roadblocks, efficiencies, and even key strategic decisions that must be made to keep the overall CDE transformation on schedule.

Most of these barriers to adoption will repeat themselves over and over as each company manages its own journey. Therefore, the organization in the early planning stages should proactively reach out to firms who are further along, experienced consultants, and others to identify best practices and templates for change that recognize the complexities and likely roadblocks. The Task Force should work diligently to eliminate the roadblocks and barriers to changes as early as possible in the process.

### *Developing Critical Skills: Problem Solving*

As stated in earlier chapters, critical skills in problem solving are vital and often (usually) represent an underdeveloped skill set in organizations. Leadership must recognize these deficits and compensate carefully to ensure that the Challenges are well designed, that they align with important and strategic goals, and that the results are tangible and measurable. Consider building and adopting a methodology and developing training curriculum. New hires should be screened for critical reasoning skills. Some staff may show particular promise in identifying and formulating problems (Challenges) and could be candidates for shared resource pools to support the broader CDE efforts in the organization.

## Engage Innovation, HR, and Business Development Functions Early

As we've said, strategy and orchestration are the fundamental areas where real value is created in the network model; accordingly, business functions such as innovation, HR, and business development have particularly important roles to play in support of the transformation. Although every part of the organization will require examination and potentially restructuring, these three areas will be specifically discussed here.

First among these is the innovation function, the lifeblood of many organizations. Encompassed by this term are business innovation, product development, traditional research and development; even marketing, creativity, and inventiveness are necessary ingredients to beating out the competition. Innovation too often measures itself by the number of strategists, researchers, patents, or the number of product development centers under construction. Instead, it should focus on understanding which problems and opportunities matter to the business. The mindset must change from running experiments to developing, finding, and exploiting solutions. Now these organizations will continue to require staff sufficient to manage the business to be sure, but the focus and overall profile may change considerably. So these organizations must build up skills in program management, partner orchestration, problem definition, and vendor relations. It must provide oversight and leadership to what are often complex programs. In some cases, these organizations will become systems integrators.

Innovation leadership may require new management tools, including options analysis and financial modeling. Most dramatically, you must be a portfolio manager and "network" orchestrator, whose only measure of success is enabling the company and its products to dominate its markets to enhance shareholder value.

HR similarly is redefined in this model. As previously discussed, this role is more strategic than ever and must now enable access to talent on a global scale in a world where people and skills are accessed on-demand. HR must be both a thought leader and the agent provocateur in areas ranging from how best to manage variable versus fixed labor costs to how the organization can tap virtual communities, including customers, retirees, and innovation markets. HR is now front and center as the organization identifies opportunities to virtualize its business model to remain competitive.

The last area highlighted is business development, which plays an increasingly core role as an enabler in the network model. Already expert in identifying value creating opportunities between business partners and structuring mutually beneficial engagement models, this function is more vital than ever. The importance of this function is apparent in organizations such as Procter & Gamble, who now places portions of their open innovation programs under powerful new global business development functions to drive efficiency and focus.

And leaders in these areas must now be evangelists and key lieutenants in driving the transformational change as they lead their departments with newly expanded charters.

### Assess Compensation and Incentive Systems Top to Bottom

Plan to completely overhaul position descriptions, goals, and compensation design. There must be an unwavering focus on shareholder value and it should drive measurement and compensation systems for all staff at all levels. Most staff cannot tie their execution to dividends and share price directly, not because it is impossible, but because we too often lack the discipline. Even building the basic linkage between individual responsibilities and key stated corporate strategies is shockingly lacking in most organizations. These systems must be realigned to drive the transformation needed.

New goals and targets should be created that track and reward progress against key transformational elements of the agenda. Goals like percent of innovation from the outside, or proportion of variable versus fixed spend, or amount of capital freed up for investment in programs are all good examples of targets that can be established.

This work should begin early and be performed in a coordinated fashion across the organization with the goal of formalizing the objectives and quickly cascading them throughout the enterprise. Identifying opportunities to redefine roles consistent with needs of the organization is part of this work. New skills and capabilities will be needed and many roles, titles, and responsibilities will change across the organization.

### Recognition Systems and Behavioral Change

Traditional and nontraditional recognition systems can have a powerful impact on behavior, including performance appraisals, compensation and incentive structures, and special recognition programs such as a President's Club. Use these tools liberally to encourage adoption.

Again, do not underestimate an organization's resolve to protect the status quo, a natural reaction to change that is difficult in any organization. Anticipate push back and work to resolve early. Be particularly vigilant in identifying pockets of passive aggression that are difficult to spot but that can have toxic implications for the success of the program. For example, actual research has shown that in some cases, open innovation test projects were selected teams by product teams with a low likelihood of success to increase likelihood of failure in order to generate negative proof points to protect the status quo.

# VII. Select Enablers and Enroll Partners

This section discusses the role of technology and partners in enabling CDE and ensuring its successful realization. We have discussed commitment, strategy, trials and adoption, and even the leadership needed in support of implementation. However, it is often difficult for organizations to change from within without enablers and partners to assist in the work ahead. Enabling technology, management consultants, trusted partners, and the like improve the odds and help in avoiding unnecessary pitfalls—not unlike the health-minded individual who chooses a gym and a personal trainer to achieve the goals that he could likely accomplish on his own. He knows the right tools can improve the odds and positively impact time to results.

Depending on the needs of the organization, several opportunities may exist to support change through tools and other enablers. A number are discussed next.

### Methodology and Training

In this context, methodology refers to having a well-defined and documented approach, complete with best practices, templates, case studies, and training modules. InnoCentive's Challenge Driven Innovation approach is an example. More general-purpose methodologies also exist in areas that address open innovation, change management, cultural change, and business process outsourcing, to name a few. Assess these methodologies and select one or more for deployment. Typically organizations will train and certify individuals, teams, and areas of their business on its use. There are scale economies here, and the greater the percentage of the organization using the methodology, the greater the benefits that can accrue. Creating a common language alone is valuable, but many of the methodologies provide much more, including management tools, measurement and analytics, best practices, and so on. Choose well and then immerse the company in its use.

Mass adoption of methodologies, technology, and processes require a programmatic approach to facilitate adoption and utilization. In the early stages, the focus should be on key leaders and practitioners who will be involved in early trial activities in addition to resources being set aside within the CDE task force, but ultimately a significant share of the overall staff should have exposure to the key concepts, tools, and so on.

HR and corporate training have roles to play here in addition to resources experienced in change management. The organization may also engage outside training firms, management consultants, and other resources to assist as needed. These programs should be integrated into existing programs, new employee training, internal certifications, and compliance programs both to attain efficiencies and to reinforce that the content is now part of the core learnings for effective employees. Large organizations may consider their own CDE University where content can be stylized based upon level and domains.

Sustaining the focus and competencies is critical. Depending on the roles, staff should be encouraged to keep its knowledge bases current. These can be done through refresher courses and reinforced by promoting communities of practice. Organizing in a symposia format can be particularly engaging for mid- and senior-level leaders and managers. For example, senior manufacturing leadership can be trained in examples relevant to their domains while also creating their own informal communities of practice. Coupled with use of intranet sites, discussion boards, and internal working papers, the knowledge, language, and capability building can be easily sustained.

### Open Innovation and Other Partnering Opportunities

CDE is built around fundamental principles, and one of those is that business can sustain themselves only through agility, innovation, and financial flexibility. Their costs of innovation continue to increase, often faster than the revenue line, while the competition is increasingly nimble. Increasingly costly and inefficient innovation organizations represent a particularly intriguing reengineering opportunity through open innovation.

Open innovation companies such as InnoCentive already have tools, methodologies, and even global innovation networks available on demand for companies. Management consultants such as Accenture and Monitor Group have dedicated innovation practices with considerable experience in organizational design, change management, and even business process reengineering. Partners such as these can significantly "de-risk" the value proposition and costs for businesses. You need to evaluate the landscape, identifying vendors and partners with potential to enable the CDE journey, and forging the partnering relationships to manage and sustain the change.

# Timelines and the Institutionalization of the CDE

Remember the term *e-business*? Used mostly in the 1990s, it had particular usefulness as businesses tried to think through how technology and global networks would impact them. Interestingly, almost with a whimper, the term fell out of use. It was not that the principles were withdrawn from the marketplace or that they were discredited— quite the contrary. The concepts became pervasive, the toolsets matured, and success stories entered the history books. In other words: *e-business* became just *business*.

This is the institutionalization needed by corporations as they engage the future. With their business models virtualized, they will be assembling and disassembling assets to capitalize on market opportunities, building global ecosystems to extend their reach and amplify their resources, and engaging millions to drive breakthrough innovation to get that next generation network router to market before the competition. At some point, the CDE must become simply how you do business.

We believe that CEOs and Boards of Directors should assume 5 to 10 years are necessary for the transformation to fully take hold, although efforts may be generating dividends to the top and bottom line much sooner. Institutionalization means that the organization isn't applying these principles because they've made commitments to the CDE task force or to finance—it is because they are practitioners and disciples of the new management science. In 5 to 10 years, cultures, people, and organizations can change dramatically.

## Use the Playbook, Adapt as Needed, and Play to Win

This playbook is designed to structure your thinking, organize your actions, and focus your efforts. It may also provide other kinds of benefits such as a basic language and project management framework for charting the approach. It contains all the basic organizing elements to begin and substantially manage the journey to becoming the CDE. Depending on the CEO and his leadership style and the company and its culture, the plays can be adapted to suit various approaches.

For example, consider these three basic approaches:

- **Transformation:** The CEO announces and launches an effort to transform the company; the future (and the present) demands it.
- **Evolutionary, not Revolutionary, Change:** The CEO makes "Open" a core value and challenges the organization to embrace its use.
- **Strategic Capability Building:** The CEO instructs the organization to "implement" CDE much like Six Sigma or Total Quality Management.

There are many levels of commitment and approach. The plays support each with simple variation of sequence, timing, and emphasis. Further, you can freely adapt the CDE Playbook to support implementation in different contexts. By making logical substitutions and applying common sense, the playbook will apply for divisions, departments, small business, government, and even the Not-for-Profit (NFP) sector.

Transformational change on any scale is difficult. Expect setbacks along the way, but seek every opportunity to learn through the process. Don't be afraid to experiment and revise the plans based upon the learnings. Invest in practices that are working and reset those that are not. Add to the playbook as institutional learnings and best practices emerge. But at all times, persevere and never withdraw from the commitment to change.

Finally, the CDE Playbook alone cannot transform the organization. A thoughtful approach is necessary but not sufficient to ensure success. Again quoting the famous football legend:

> "Coaches who can outline plays on a blackboard are a dime a dozen. The ones who win get inside their players and motivate."
>
> —*Vince Lombardi*

Lombardi was not advising coaches to throw away the playbooks. Instead he was talking about the real vision and leadership required to make magic happen. That is the topic of the last chapter.

# Case Study: How the Prize4Life Foundation Is Crowdsourcing ALS Research

At age 29, Avi Kremer was diagnosed with ALS (Amyotrophic Lateral Sclerosis, also known as Lou Gehrig's disease). "What do I do now?" he asked his doctor. "Prepare a will," the doctor replied.[2]

ALS is a rare disease, striking 2 out of 100,000 people, usually between the ages of 40–70. Not only is there no known cure for ALS, but there is only one FDA-approved treatment that is only modestly effective Most patients die within 2–5 years of diagnosis. On top of that, accurate diagnosis is often elusive and difficult. Avi himself was misdiagnosed twice by doctors who attributed his symptoms of uncontrollable hand cramps and inability to lift the same weights as before to "stress" and pronounced him "in great health," before he was correctly diagnosed.[3]

Although its cause is unknown, ALS' symptoms are torturously similar: a progressive loss of all motor control, beginning with the hands, feet, speech centers, and eventually even to control of breathing itself. All the while, however, the mind typically remains perfectly intact and sharp, trapped inside the totally paralyzed body.

As Avi researched the disease and his options, he began to realize that the doctor's advice to "make a will" was truly one of the few concrete steps open to him as an ALS sufferer. There were no medications to delay or ameliorate the symptoms except one drug, which prolonged life at most 2–3 months at a cost prohibitive to many payers.

But Avi, a former Captain in the Israeli army who had just been admitted to Harvard Business School two months before his diagnosis, decided to do more than just make a will. He decided to apply all his training, brainpower, and resources available to him at Harvard to make the biggest impact he could on the development of treatments and possibly even a cure for ALS. His first tack: to figure out why more wasn't being done in ALS drug development? The answers here proved easy to find. First, ALS was a rare disease—only a total of 640,000 people worldwide have it. Second, those patients who do have ALS die quickly, meaning it is difficult to recruit enough patients to run large clinical trials. Third, because the disease's cause was not known and there were no biomarkers to evaluate its progression, the main way to tell if a given therapy had value was to see whether patients lived or died, leading to long clinical trials. The upshot of these three factors was that while the market was attractive, ALS clinical trials were difficult, expensive, and risky. So how could this be changed? As Avi examined his options for the few years of life left to him, he saw he could:

- raise money for ALS research, as Michael J. Fox has done for Parkinson's Disease.
- launch a drug company that would pursue a promising therapy.
- offer a prize, à la the Ansari X PRIZE, to the first person or team to make a step toward a cure.

The idea for the third option came from a class that Avi attended, where Jill Panetta, then Chief Scientific Officer at InnoCentive, had spoken about the role of prizes in spurring research and solutions in a given area. For example, the Ansari X PRIZE had given birth to the commercial space industry by offering a $10 million prize to the first team from private industry to devise a spacecraft capable of carrying three people 100 kilometers above the earth twice within two weeks.

Avi wanted to do something similar for ALS, and he formed the Prize4Life Foundation to do just that. Prize4Life would award $1 million to the first person or team that identified and validated an ALS biomarker (a way to track disease progression) that could be used to de-risk ALS clinical trials.

The prize approach had several advantages. First, it would bring attention and a laser-like focus to the specific need for a clinically relevant ALS biomarker (a critical missing tool in the drug development landscape). Second, the prize presented a novel way to get funding for the disease—donors would only pay if the prize were awarded. This appealed to an entrepreneurial class of donors, attracting new sources of money to the field. Third, the prize would be global, meaning that anyone from anywhere in the world could compete for it. This unique aspect of the prize model, to incentivize individuals and teams from diverse disciplines to consider how to translate their expertise to the challenge of ALS, supported InnoCentive's previous experience that with seemingly intractable problems, solutions often come from someone outside the field.. Finally, the publicity around the prize—the largest that Prize4Life partner InnoCentive had ever offered at the time—would help generate increased awareness for the disease.

Prize4Life put a two-year end date on its prize award—an extremely aggressive timeline. "It can often take a researcher two years just to get an NIH grant funded," said Melanie Leitner, Ph.D., Chief Scientific Officer at Prize4Life. Nonetheless, Prize4Life's Scientific Advisory Board believed that despite the very high bar, there was a reasonable likelihood that it could be met in two years. "Given the urgency of the need it, was worth taking the risk," Leitner said.

More than 50 teams from 18 countries competed for the prize, and 12 submissions were received by the deadline. "We have often said that one of the best things the incentive prize model can do is attract a wide variety of people to think about a particular problem in new and different ways, and the submissions we received demonstrate that, as a complement to front-end funding and support, the prize model can truly help accelerate the discovery of answers to very focused problems," Leitner said.

At the end of two years, no team had met all the criteria for the prize, but two were very close: a dermatologist with no previous ALS research experience, and a long-time ALS researcher who decided to narrow his focus specifically to the ALS biomarker challenge. Given how close the two had come to solving the challenge, Prize4Life awarded both solvers $50,000 Progress Prizes to reward their efforts to date and reissued the prize for another two years.

"If this Challenge hadn't been issued, there is little chance I would have even pursued this idea," said the dermatologist, Dr. Harvey Arbesman. "This approach has been an effective way to get people across disciplines, from all around the world, to think about ALS and has been an effective way to tap new perspectives from outside the field. I am greatly encouraged by the results of our research thus far and am hopeful it will have a positive impact on ALS treatment in the future."

Seward Rutkove, the other Progress Prize winner, said, "When I became aware of the Challenge, I had already been pursuing this very research in neurological diseases for several years. In a way it was a lucky coincidence, but participating in the Challenge helped to refine my thinking. It led me to apply my technology research specifically to ALS focusing on both the animal studies and device development. In our case, participation has effectively sped the development of a handheld device to sensitively measure disease progression."

A year later, Rutkove submitted a revised proposal based on his additional research and work. Prize4Life's independent Scientific Advisory Board unanimously agreed that Rutkove had met all the criteria of the challenge. He had identified a clinically relevant biomarker of disease progression and was awarded $1 million.

Although $1 million is a big prize, it is a very small price to pay for the discovery, and it highlights the productivity of the prize approach. "The Alzheimer's Disease field has recently seen major progress in the identification of useful clinical biomarkers, but this has followed an enormous financial investment (over $100 million) in the form of the ADNI consortium, which was initiated in 2004," Leitner said. "The Parkinson's Disease field has also just initiated a $40+ million effort to identify new Parkinson's Disease biomarkers."

Going forward, Prize4Life will continue offering specific prizes for specific solutions. "We believe in the model. The right prize for the right question can lead to major breakthroughs," Leitner said.

Avi added, "Prizes are risk-free; you only pay for what you want."

The bottom line? In a relatively short time and at much lower cost than traditional research, Prize4Life is proving that open innovation and incentive prizes can be a very powerful toolset to accelerate breakthroughs in even the most complex areas of R&D.

# 9 ————————————————

# Leadership

"A hero is someone who has given his or her life to something bigger than oneself."
—*Joseph Campbell in* The Power of Myth

## Overview

With this book, you have the key concepts, learnings, decision tools, case studies, and even a playbook to follow. However, even with these tools, many leaders will be too risk averse to make the difficult choices for reasons already discussed. Or they will delay until externalities demand action, possibly after it is already too late. The transformational change described requires genuine vision and courage. Make no mistake, this will test leadership and organizations to their limits, but the near and long-term gains could be extraordinary.

This, the final chapter, is written for the CEOs, leaders, and decision makers contemplating this course for their organizations. We will examine the inescapable need for change in this fast-paced, global, hyper-competitive twenty-first century. And we will explore the unique and profound role of the CEO and key leadership in bringing the Challenge Driven Enterprise to life, invoking Joseph Campbell's *The Hero's Journey* as a guide. Finally, we will provide a few parting thoughts on the role of the CEO and legacy.

Let's begin by briefly reviewing key takeaways of the book thus far to ensure that the major points are both fresh and clear:

# Key Points of the Book

## Chapter 1: "Introduction"

Every business and undertaking is based upon probabilities and portfolio management. Bets are made every day in every corporation, whether deciding the next drug to develop in the pharmaceutical industry, building a factory, or choosing the next CEO. Understanding how to best manage those risks and maximize options is fundamental to good business management, which is particularly true in a world where constant innovation and smart risk taking is the new normal. Effective leaders must balance their resources between efforts of exploration and exploitation. Open innovation offers an enhanced toolbox for accomplishing these things. The purposes of the bets, the portfolios, and the risk management are to produce innovations that distinguish one company from another in the marketplace. To this end, all leaders must engage in meta-innovation—innovating on the way they innovate.

## Chapter 2: "The Future of Value Creation"

Economics and business management have evolved considerably over the years. The seminal work of Ronald Coase and subsequent economic theorists help you better understand why firms developed the way they did—to drive efficiency and to minimize transaction costs. But the conditions that marked the business environment as we transitioned from the nineteenth to the twentieth century are unlike those prevailing as we enter the next. This century brings with it not only a fundamental change in transaction costs, but also unprecedented pace, global markets, constant competition, connected customers, and the Internet. Businesses must re-architect themselves to drive innovation, agility, and time to market. They must rethink the metrics that guided them in the past. Value will be captured by the firms that adapt to meet the challenge.

## Chapter 3: "A New Innovation Framework"

After a century of building institutions, the innovation function is costly, inflexible, dated, and undermanaged. As leaders, you may have too readily convinced yourselves that innovation is inherently fluid and that applying any kind of process and measurement dooms the function to mediocrity, which could not be further from the truth. A channel-based approach is introduced that provides new predictability, risk management, agility, and metrics. It also capitalizes on a connected world of diverse skills lying outside the walls of the corporation. This innovation framework will be vital to new organizations and will challenge the status quo in traditional firms. Internal change will be necessary to effectively access that which is external.

## Chapter 4: "The Long Tail of Expertise"

Key to building more flexible and innovative businesses will be the recognition that creativity, ingenuity, production capacity, and even raw materials exist everywhere and that businesses own, employ, manage, or are even aware of only a tiny fraction. Modern businesses will increasingly harness a traditionally untapped cadre of innovators, collaborators, and business partners to drive clearly superior returns. Their ability to effectively access the long tail will be not only vital to continued success but also essential to survival as competitors expand their access to creativity and problem-solving potential.

## Chapter 5: "The Selection of Appropriate Innovation Channels"

Building the capabilities to engage various "channels" for innovation will be critical to future business. Posing the right problems to the right groups is a decision-making endeavor that requires understanding the capabilities, benefits, and risks of each potential channel. In some cases, multiple channels are advisable. Ultimately, effective channel and portfolio management go hand-in-hand and are the capabilities that will separate the leaders from the laggards.

## Chapter 6: "The Challenge Driven Enterprise"

After examining the "Challenge" in more detail and exploring its unique ability to structure and focus human activity, we take the concepts from earlier chapters even further and introduce the Challenge Driven Enterprise. CDE provides nothing less than a future vision for organizations to drive innovation, agility, and better economics for doing business in the twenty-first century. It enables new modes of innovation, while creating the flexibility to capitalize on new business opportunities. Inherent in this approach is a remaking of the corporation to be more lean, efficient, and flexible, which has significant implications. Industry leaders will be those that successfully apply these concepts universally, from business strategy to the manufacturing plant floor.

## Chapter 7: "Transformation"

This chapter discussed the evolution of how modern firms are organized and the evolving "network" form that is replacing it. The powerful role of corporate culture in supporting or resisting the transformation is examined as well as the intense effort that goes into building new organizational structures. Key considerations for CEOs and business leaders are identified as they contemplate the change ahead. The level of effort and dedication required for most organizations should not be underestimated.

## Chapter 8:" The Challenge Driven Enterprise Playbook"

Essential strategies and tactics are brought together as a "playbook" to enable business leaders to initiate the transformation. Although every organization is different and at various stages in their evolution, the essential elements of a structured and comprehensive program are detailed, including: securing commitment, promoting early trial and adoption, virtualizing business strategy, establishing the CEO mandate, empowering the CDE Task Force, readying the organization, and selecting enablers and partners.

### *Chapter 9: "Leadership"*

And as mentioned in the introduction to this chapter, we will now focus on the role of leadership and, in particular, the epic journey on which they and their organizations must travel to truly transform.

# Darwin, Adaptation, and the New Normal

No one knows for sure why the dinosaurs disappeared 65 million years ago, but what is clear is that their time had come. Perhaps bigger was no longer better. Whatever the reason, their evolutionary path did not prepare them to overcome the calamity that struck. Smaller, more agile life did survive to reset the food chain. Birds today may actually be direct descendants of dinosaurs. Darwin wasn't kidding when he suggested "survival of the fittest" and dinosaurs as they existed were no longer viable. Many corporations are modern-day dinosaurs, but they have significant advantages over their Cretaceous namesakes—they wield considerable freedom to operate as well as the unique ability to contemplate the future. In other words, they can *choose* to adapt to new challenges in front of them.

The business landscape has changed, and there will be no turning back of the clocks. The institutions that we've built over decades or centuries have enabled massive scale and efficiency and have served us well. But while the modern corporation was a masterpiece, it is rapidly losing ground to more agile and innovative forms of business. A confluence of enablers, which include globalization, outsourcing, standards, 24/7 services, and universal connectivity, has ushered in a new era of virtual business in which the innovative and agile prosper. Senior leadership has an existential choice to make. Rather than deny the new business realities, they should embrace them, recognizing that the future holds great promise for firms willing to adapt. The new normal is constant competition and a pace that is unprecedented. Established firms must now evolve.

But evolution for business is about change. And that change impacts people, culture, practices, and systems. It requires considerable commitment, thoughtful planning, real dedication, and substantial resources. Most importantly, it requires unwavering and inspired CEO-level leadership to preside over a difficult and lengthy process of transformation. This is a heroic journey and one that may not be taken lightly.

## Joseph Campbell and *The Hero's Journey*

A renowned scholar and writer, Joseph Campbell has impacted both our understanding of culture and our culture itself. He has influenced fields ranging from anthropology to psychology. And his writings, beginning with the 1949 publishing of *The Hero with a Thousand Faces*, famously introduced *The Hero's Journey*.

Throughout civilization, myths have aided individuals and peoples to understand and relate to the world around them, natural and supernatural. They speak to the trials and tribulations inherent in human existence and sometimes attempt to deal with the truly cosmic questions: Why are we here? Can one person make a difference? Campbell studied many cultures and their stories and recognized that a strikingly formulaic and consistent pattern emerges going back to ancient myths including *Beowulf* and *The Odyssey*. In each case, the hero has a call to adventure, receives aid or guidance, must face life or death situations, endures trials and temptations, transforms into the hero, seeks atonement, and returns home victorious. He called this pattern the Monomyth. Following the pattern, modern heroes emerge as well in books and movies, such as Neo in the *Matrix* or Luke Skywalker in the *Star Wars* saga, for which George Lucas credited Campbell as the true inspiration.

These myths talk to who we are as a people. They give us meaning and guidance, delineate the light from the darkness, and inspire us to be more than we are. The archetype is of course not random; it is actually a remarkably approachable metaphor for life and transformation. But there is another learning to be derived from the metaphor. We know the names of Homer and Luke Skywalker, but what of the countless others that never answered the call to adventure? We'll never know their names. They missed their opportunity. What of those that tried and failed? We may not know their names either. But what is clear is that leaders have accepted great responsibility and must live up to that responsibility. And nothing extraordinary happens without taking risk.

We invoke the hero's journey to provide a frame for comprehending the magnitude of the implications inherent in committing to the Challenge Driven Enterprise and the enormous resolve required to see the transformation through to its conclusion. In truth, few of our leaders will live up to their true potential because most will fall short at that pivotal moment when the difficult choices must be made and real leadership exhibited. But some will emerge as true heroes, returning home victorious. Whether they are remaking IBM, launching a new industry, or bringing down the Berlin Wall, our great leaders travel their own hero's journey. They see the challenges in front of them and answer the call, impacting the fortunes of thousands or millions of people as a result. They persevere against formidable odds and triumph over those that would have them fail. The strength of their resolve and the boundless commitment to the vision will inspire many to follow. And in so doing, they impact generations and leave behind legacies.

So how can we more practically translate the hero's journey to a modern business context? Let's consider the intellectual progression required by the CEO contemplating CDE and the change ahead. Keeping with the metaphor, we describe the progression in terms of waypoints along the CEO's journey.

# The CEOs Journey: Five Essential Waypoints

The CEO's journey includes five essential waypoints or stops along the way: Realization, Vision, Decision, Action, and Resolve. They represent conscious stages in the CEOs journey as well as the logical and intellectual progression in which they are realized. For example, Realization must precede Vision or the latter will lack boldness and the essential force of urgency and conviction. Let's now discuss each in turn.

## I. Realization

The CEO must clearly recognize and accept that all the rules have changed. Global hyper-competitive markets set the new pace. Agile, networked, innovative, "open," and lean are attributes of the new normal. And this is both a wakeup call and a profound opportunity on which to capitalize. In some cases, the business may already be approaching the abyss. In others, it may be the visionary CEO recognizing changes coming to his industry years in advance and boldly positioning the firm out in front. Either way, the recognition is absolute. The real question now is "How must we evolve?"

## II. Vision

In increasingly dynamic and competitive industries, vision, strategic purpose, and focus must remain clear and compelling, even though modes of value creation and capture may change dramatically. The CEO must have a simple, clear, and bold vision of the future that comprehends network orchestration, lean practices, constant change, and the entire scope of concepts discussed in this book. But to be clear, the vision must comprehend not only changing customer demands, and a highly competitive environment, but also how the organization will be structured to compete efficiently and effectively well into the future. It must conform to the concepts and drivers underlying CDE.

For example, Local Motors represents true disruption in the well-established automotive industry and provides yet another wakeup call to this struggling sector. Growing concern with fossil fuels and the continued urbanization of the planet are "mega trends" that must be considered. Reimagining companies and industries is an example of an enormous undertaking, but it is one that essential. Amazon redefined retail. Proctor & Gamble embraced open innovation years before their competition. Google reinvented online search and the advertising scheme to monetize it. We must do this in all our industries. If you do not have a bold and compelling vision of the future, rest assured someone else will.

## III. Decision

After the leader has recognized the need for change and assembled a compelling vision of the future comes the real moment of truth. It is the singular and fully committed decision to drive a profound and irreversible transformation in order to execute on the vision. With the possible exception of testing components of the approach on a smaller scale to gain early learnings, there are no half measures. This is a monumental decision and one that must be made with purpose and conviction. When made, there is no turning back. Unfortunately, it would be too easy to suggest that making the decision is the most difficult step, because execution is even harder.

## IV. Action

The chief executive must now bring this program to life. Transformation on this scale requires focus, precision, intensity, and perseverance, particularly when executing against an agenda that may span several years, if not the tenure of multiple CEOs. There will be significant demands of the CEO, senior team, and the entire organization and the stresses on the firm will be considerable. Business lines and functions will be reengineered. Jobs will be created and lost. Mistakes will be made. Making the success of this program a mandate and ultimately a legacy, the CEO must now "own" this program and take ultimate responsibility for the transformation.

### V. Resolve

Seeing the transformation through will require incredible resolve. This will not be an easy journey, and the temptation to slow or turn back the program will appear at every turn. It is the resolve and the unshakeable commitment to change that will fuel the transformation. It should be noted that resolve here is manifest in a variety of ways and certain choices may ease or complicate the burden of resolve down the road. For example, deciding to reallocate resources from lackluster programs to CDE initiatives very early on will accelerate the realization of benefits while creating organizational acceptance and building momentum.

In Joseph Campbell's terms, these first three waypoints represent answering the call to adventure, and the two remaining are more about seeing the journey through to its final epic conclusion, overcoming every obstacle along the way.

## The CEO as the Hero

In modern times, chief executives (of a business or a country) often spend their entire lives in pursuit of the office. This is a journey in which few succeed. And it is fraught with its own challenges and setbacks. Often, incredible prowess and skill is necessary at each step along the way to progress. There should be no doubt about the measure of the accomplishment.

For our purposes, the journey doesn't end with accepting the title and charge, it actually begins. Whether it is accepting the oath to be the President of the United States or one's primary fiduciary responsibility to shareholders as a company director or CEO, our leaders are in a unique position to change everything...or not to have any impact at all. They choose to be the steward, the change agent, or the chief executive. Few in the world have both free will *and* the resources to have impact. These individual have both, but what will they do with that awesome responsibility?

Modern-day leaders may see the opportunity to enter new markets or execute on a game-changing acquisition as a call to adventure. They are less likely to view remaking the firm in that same light. Adventure here refers to entering into the unknown, taking risks, and taking control of one's (or the company's) future. Often in the Monomyth, the hero will refuse the call initially. This, of course, is emblematic of the classical leader in organizations where, as we've discussed, the very institutions we've created have trained us to avoid real risks. We fail to recognize the sign or dismiss outright the call to adventure as too prone to failure. Or we'll rationalize away the need to take truly bold action. Too often, we'll simply leave the tough decisions to the next in line for succession, which may have no choice but to act. There will be many trials along the way for the CEO who has accepted the call, including constant questions from Wall Street that test the CEO's resolve. Every setback will be cause for rolling back the agenda. The hero's journey demands that each of these be dealt with as the story progresses.

Metaphorically, neither dragons nor sirens may stand in the way of what must be done nor sway the hero from the path chosen. There must be a death and rebirth of sorts. Virtualizing the firm, remaking the enterprise, and reimagining lines of business *are and should be acts of destruction and creation*—the CEO and the company will transform and be transformed by the experience.

So powerful is the link between the hero and the journey, the CEO and the transformation, that they cannot be easily isolated. And neither should we try. The story of IBM's legendary transformation and Lou Gerstner's leadership are one and the same. One cannot imagine describing Proctor & Gamble's journey without A.G. Lafley at its center. Transformation is an epic journey, and epic journeys like myth require heroes...or at least heroic leadership. But realize that we all have that hint of hero inside us. That is what the hero's journey teaches us. It is the will to make the tough decisions and the follow through that separates Homer from the others. Now we will leave the discussion of myth and metaphor and briefly mention timescale and expectations.

# A Marathon, Not a Sprint

Rome was not built in a day. The difficulty with any major change management effort is not simply in making the tough decisions that launch the initiatives; it is in staying the course. At every turn, leadership will be challenged to delay key milestones, to soften expectations, to identify exceptions to the program, and to put top executives "on more pressing matters." They will be accused of pushing too hard, putting the business at risk, even acting out of pride. Most change management efforts fail. They fail for many reasons, including poor planning, lack of resources, poor sponsorship, long time horizons, and so on. But there is a theme underlying the majority of failure, and it is poorly set expectations and the lack of resolve over realistic time horizons. Leadership must commit to change and see the initiative through to its conclusion—efforts that will span years.

In his book *Who Says Elephants Can't Dance*, Lou Gerstner discussed the recognition that after he stabilized IBM in the 1990s, the real challenge was whether to be a mediocre company or to rise again to lead an industry. Gerstner said "The sprint was over. Our marathon was about to begin." Transformation, whether turning around a juggernaut and industry icon like IBM or remaking a midsized company that has simply lost its edge, requires a significant commitment, patience, and a substantial amount of time on the part of the Board, CEO, senior leadership, investors, employees, and others. Make no mistake: The transformation to becoming a Challenge Driven Enterprise is a marathon. Be realistic in setting expectations and enroll the organization for the long haul.

# The CDE, Innovation, and Competing in the Twenty-First Century

The Challenge Driven Enterprise is a far-reaching vision with profound implications. It will transform organizations in every sense of the word. They will become more agile, innovative, and competitive, enabling better capital flexibility and financial performance. Networks, ecosystems, and lean operations replace hierarchy, mass, and bureaucracy. This is a business evolution already underway, being driven by dynamics well beyond the scope of any one business, industry, or nation (see discussion of Thomas Friedman's the *World Is Flat* in Chapter 2). Competition is fierce, and new business formation is constant and requires astonishingly little in the way of hard assets, full-time employees, or overhead as we know it. Meanwhile customer loyalty and switching costs are evaporating rapidly. CDE recognizes these dynamics and challenges your organization to embrace and capitalize on the change rather than falling victim to it. The CDE is a flexible vision and one that can be stylized to nearly any business.

If upstarts are beating you to market with better products and fresher ideas, you are losing customers and your innovation edge. If capital is tied up in dated and expensive factories while the competition is contracting manufacturing capacity from state-of-the-art facilities at lower costs, you are bloated and inflexible. If you are turning away business opportunities because your culture simply cannot adapt, you need to evolve.

Peter Drucker is famously quoted as saying that the singular purpose of business is to generate customers and that only two functions do this: marketing and innovation. All the rest are simply costs. Now Drucker meant marketing in a broad sense, not simply demand generation. And he also meant innovation in a larger sense, not simply R&D. The power of Drucker's statement is its pure, simple recognition that customers must be "made" in order to create value and that nothing else matters in business.

We have introduced our own version of simplicity in this book. Businesses have two functions that matter in the new economy: strategy and network orchestration. What will you do to create value? How can you win in a world where virtual networks and global ecosystems replace scale and bureaucracy? How will you adapt to a new normal that is characterized by dynamic business environments and increasingly aggressive, innovative, and lean competition? What both views of the world share is that much of the work in today's companies, from repetitive tasks to the most inventive acts of product development, can be distributed, virtualized, or outsourced—yielding more efficient and competitive businesses and freeing up capital and resources to capture that next billion dollar opportunity. When it can be better performed elsewhere, it generally should be. Significant gains and advantages will be realized by focusing on what creates profitable customers and in creating and capturing value for our companies and stakeholders. These two views actually reconcile perfectly in that regard. However, most companies today must evolve and transform radically if they are going to continue to lead and win in their sectors. The Challenge Driven Enterprise provides a framework.

For most businesses and leaders, the next step is a choice with profound significance: Maintain the status quo or adapt to the new realities of competition. The business journals are filled with stories of struggling or defunct companies such as Blockbuster, Circuit City, and Fannie Mae, many of which were highlighted as *Good to Great* companies in the book by the same name. These organizations failed to anticipate structural changes or the impact of new competition. And the notion that no company is too big to fail has been thoroughly discredited by the last financial crisis. The only constant is change. For most firms, CDE transformation (or an equivalent) represents the only sensible strategy to competing in the new economy.

# This Will Be Your Legacy

As mentioned and reinforced throughout this book, the CEOs' role is to build and sustain enduring and profitable enterprises to create and capture value. We live in a dynamic global economy where products are delivered at a breakneck pace, where new business ideas can go from concept to scale overnight, and where shocks to the economy can result in the destruction of companies previously thought too big to fail. Competition is fierce. Businesses are at a breaking point and the landscape is evolving quickly—and it is unforgiving. The Challenge Driven Enterprise is an encompassing business vision that provides a roadmap for businesses to adapt and transform. Those that adopt this approach will have a unique opportunity to operate more efficiently and effectively than ever before, tapping an entire world of innovation, capabilities, and business opportunity.

The choice to implement this approach is not to be taken lightly. We invoked the hero's journey to paint a picture through metaphor of what, for many leaders and organizations, is to be an epic journey. You might ask whether the envisioned transformation is potentially too large to manage. Is it even possible on this scale? We've already discussed adoption of some of the principles in large and complex firms. And as you will see in the final case study, President Obama is striving to remake the U.S. government, essentially the oldest, largest, and most complex American enterprise, as open, participatory, and collaborative. Bold and visionary works on every scale!

For leaders with the vision, courage, and tenacity, not only will you remake your businesses for the twenty-first century, you will also leave a lasting legacy. Welch, Gerstner, Lafley, and others before were strong leaders who left an enduring imprint. Their actions have ensured competitiveness for their organizations for decades to come;

and rest assured they have created enormous value for their shareholders in the process. You will be the inspiration and guiding hand
that transforms the bureaucratic, bloated, industrial era corporation
into one that competes in and dominates its segments in the new age.
IBM changed. P&G remade its future. President Obama is resetting
government. Commit to the transformation needed and lead with
purpose and resolve. This will be your legacy.

# Case Study: How President Obama's Open Government Initiative Is Reinventing Government and Changing Culture

On his first full day in office, President Obama declared a new
level of openness for the government:

> My Administration is committed to creating an unprece-
> dented level of openness in Government. We will work
> together to ensure the public trust and establish a system of
> transparency, public participation, and collaboration. Open-
> ness will strengthen our democracy and promote efficiency
> and effectiveness in Government.
>
> President Barack Obama, January 21, 2009[1]

He issued a memorandum to all heads of executive departments
and agencies outlining his vision for transparency, participation, and
collaboration, and announcing the Open Government Initiative:

- **Government should be participatory:** Public engagement
  enhances the government's effectiveness and improves the
  quality of its decisions. Knowledge is widely dispersed in society, and public officials benefit from having access to that dispersed knowledge. Executive departments and agencies should
  offer Americans increased opportunities to participate in poli-
  cymaking and to provide their government with the benefits of
  their collective expertise and information. Executive departments and agencies should also solicit public input on how we
  can increase and improve opportunities for public participation
  in government.

- **Government should be collaborative:** Collaboration actively engages Americans in the work of their government. Executive departments and agencies should use innovative tools, methods, and systems to cooperate among themselves, across all levels of government, and with nonprofit organizations, businesses, and individuals in the private sector. Executive departments and agencies should solicit public feedback to assess and improve their level of collaboration and to identify new opportunities for cooperation.[2]

Obama's phrase that "knowledge is widely dispersed in society" raised the question, "How do we capture the insights of the American people?" White House Chief Technology Officer Aneesh Chopra said, "In traditional environments, it's difficult, but with the use of today's technologies, crowdsourcing platforms, and others, we can find that needle in the haystack and bring those ideas to fruition." Speaking at the Personal Democracy Forum 2010, Chopra described an example and its results: "I share with you the results of NASA's early experience with the InnoCentive scientific expert network platform, a platform of roughly 200,000 scientists, where NASA said we're going to pose a few difficult scientific challenges. One of which was 'how can we forecast solar activity so we can better predict when and how we should release our rockets into space?'" This was a vexing problem that NASA had been grappling with for more than 30 years. By putting the challenge out to the public, a semi-retired radio frequency engineer living in rural New Hampshire had the opportunity to share his idea on how to address the problem. As Chopra said, all the engineer needed "was an Internet connection. No complicated RPF, the need for a lobbyist, some convoluted process—just a smart person in our country who could help solve a difficult scientific challenge and was paid a modest $30,000 for that insight."[3]

Beyond the innovation spurred by the Open Government Directive, numerous nonpartisan institutions praised the directive for its commitment on Obama's campaign. For example, Ellen Miller, director of the nonpartisan Sunlight Foundation, said that Obama followed through on his promise: "The Open Government Directive issued today demonstrates the seriousness of the administration's commitment to data transparency and citizen engagement. It is evidence that the administration recognizes that transparency is government's responsibility. At the same time, it shows the administration is matching aspirational goals with concrete policies and accountability measures."[4]

Likewise, Gary Bass, executive director of OMB Watch, praised the White House: "The directive's scope and specificity blends both rigorous timelines and agency flexibility that will likely achieve significant improvements in government openness across agencies."[5]

Bass added, however, "The key will be how the public, the White House, and federal agencies work together in implementing the directive." Bass' comment hints at one of the obstacles Obama, like any CEO, faces: overcoming resistance to change.

The federal government millions of staffers, so change won't come quickly or easily. There are generational issues and positional ones. For example, Staff Sgt. Joshua Salmons, emerging media coordinator at the Defense Information School said, "Junior troops, operationally, are doing all this stuff already. They are digital natives. The senior leaders understand the value of this. It does fall to the middle sector to get onboard."[6]

To help deal with these concerns and facilitate cultural change, workshops are held on how to implement the Open Government Directive. The workshops let government officials voice concerns and work together to identify solutions. The solutions are then posted on government wikis to share the learnings: http://ogw.wikispaces.com/Government+Culture.[7]

As government employees work through these issues, tangible progress and successes are seen across the board. In strictly numerical terms, the number of data sets on Data.gov (launched in May 2009 as part of the OGI) rose from 47 in the summer of 2009 to

118,000 by December 2009, with thousands more sets released as OGI continues.[8]

The true measure of success, however, isn't just the amount of data that's available, but how that data is used by the public or by private enterprises and what value is created as a result. Following are some results so far:

**Asthmapolis:** A data platform to help patients and public health professionals track the geography of asthma attacks by attaching a real-time sensor to an inhaler that records the time and location of its use. Empowered by this information, patients may be able to avoid asthma hotspots and reduce costly hospital visits through prevention.[9]

**Apps for Healthy Kids:** The U.S. Department of Agriculture publishes a dataset about nutritional values of common foods. This enabled the First Lady to announce the "Apps for Healthy Kids" competition and challenge the "most creative, talented, and kid-savvy innovators" across the country to build games that use those data to inspire and empower kids to get active and eat healthy."[10]

Inspired by the challenge, local chapters of the International Game Developers Association organized weekend-long game jams in eight cities across the United States. The $60,000 in prizes attracted 160 entries and more than 40,000 supporters by the time the submission period closed on June 30, 2010.[11] Developers used a downloadable database on Data.gov of the nutritional information of 1,000 of the most commonly eaten foods. The apps will educate kids and their families on nutrition and making smart food choices.[12]

**Emergency Response:** Virtual USA—a collaboration among the Department of Homeland Security, the emergency response community, and eight states across the nation—is an innovative information-sharing system that helps federal, state, local, and tribal first responders work with all levels of government to make fast, well-informed decisions. The system links these partners' disparate tools and technologies to share the location and operational status of power and water lines, flood detectors, helicopter-capable landing sites, emergency vehicle and ambulance locations, weather and traffic conditions, evacuation routes, and school and government building floor plans, and does so without requiring any participating entity to change either the system it now uses or the way it does business.[13] The effort was based on solving real-world problems of local and state practitioners to manage data access within their own jurisdictions and to share information with relevant jurisdictions across the nation.[14]

In the end, Obama's goal with the Open Government Initiative is to bring in new ideas and participation that will drive collaboration and innovation:

> This Administration's commitment to public participation is based on the simple notion that many of the best ideas come from outside of Washington. While participation brings information to government so that officials can make more informed policy decisions, collaboration focuses on finding innovative strategies for solving challenges.[15]

# Afterword

We have introduced concepts both simple and complex. Sometimes building upon old ideas, we have also presented new frameworks and approaches intended to be both practical and implementable in most businesses. Our sincere goal is that you can literally transform the way you innovate and manage your business through the use of the ideas discussed in this book. As high a goal as we have attempted to hit with this book, it has been an incredibly rewarding experience for us as the authors. And we hope you derive as much from reading these chapters as we did writing them.

Family, friends, colleagues, and reviewers have all provided terrific feedback these past months, which has added immeasurably to the quality of the book and its readability. Interestingly, there were a few areas of recurring feedback that we could not address sufficiently in the book. First was the desire to tell InnoCentive's story from its founding to the present—and forward, to what might come next. Indeed the story is like no other and is one that we love to tell. The second area involves delving deeply into our learnings over the years in understanding the mechanics of inducements, prizes, and other incentives in organizing work effectively and enabling collaborative innovation on increasingly large scales—in essence, the behavioral psychology of crowdsourcing from InnoCentive's unique vantage point. The final area was the call for many more case studies telling the amazing stories of InnoCentive's solvers and their ingenuity and dedication in finding solutions to problems.

Now as we said in the introduction, this book was written to educate, tool, and even inspire leaders to embark on a journey to transform their organizations. Unfortunately, the richness of that topic meant that we used InnoCentive examples only where required to make the points needed in the book. In other words, our targeted readers required only minimal treatment of those topics, allowing us to focus more broadly on new innovation frameworks, the multiplicity of innovation channels, management issues, methodology, culture, and so forth.

That said, there is no doubt that we are at the center of a hotbed of activity that is shattering all the prior notions of how innovation happens, how organizations should access and manage talent, and why people do what they do. We observe and facilitate unbelievably inspiring stories of the power of crowds to do everything from accelerating industrial research, to imagining new business opportunities, to accelerating cures for neglected diseases. We agree. These stories may well be the basis of the next book. So stay tuned!

# Endnotes

## Foreword

1. Stan Davis and Christopher Meyer, BLUR, Addison Wesley 1998.
2. This story of Linux has been told many times, so is not repeated here.
3. BLUR, whose subtitle was "The Speed of Change in the Connected Economy," focused on the reasons for this; by now they need no explanation.

## Chapter 1

1. Henry William Chesbrough, *Open Innovation: The New Imperative for Creating and Profiting from Technology* (Boston: Harvard Business Press, 2005).
2. Tom Standage in presenting Business Innovation award to Alpheus Bingham at *The Economist* award dinner, November, 2006.
3. Jeff Howe, "The Rise of Crowdsourcing," *Wired*, no. 14.06 (June 2006), http://www.wired.com/wired/archive/14.06/crowds.html.
4. Michael E. Raynor and Jill A. Panetta, "Better Way to R&D," Harvard Business Publishing higher education newsletter, March 15, 2005, http://cb.hbsp. harvard.edu/cb/web/product_detail.seam;jsessionid=A210A06B006496915FA5 D14784E3E29F?R=S0503E-PDF-ENG&conversationId=205604&E=73043.

## Chapter 2

1. Peter F. Drucker, *Managing in the Next Society* (New York: St. Martin's Press, 2002), 68.

2. R. H. Coase, "The Nature of the Firm," Economica 4, no. 16 (November 1937): 386–405, http://www.jstor.org/pss/2626876,doi:10.1111/j.1468-0335.1937.tb00002.x.

3. Eric von Hippel, *Democratizing Innovation* (Cambridge: MIT Press, 2005).

4. Don Tapscott and Anthony D. Williams, *Wikinomics: How Mass Collaboration Changes Everything*, Expanded Edition (Portfolio Trade, 2010).

5. James Surowiecki, *The Wisdom of Crowds* (New York: Anchor Books, 2004).

6. Ibid.

7. Barry Libert, *Social Nation: How to Harness the Power of Social Media to Attract Customers, Motivate Employees, and Grow Your Business* (Wiley, 2010).

8. Ernest Hemingway, *The Sun Also Rises* (Charles Scribner's Sons, 1926).

9. John Hagel III and John Seely Brown, *The Only Sustainable Edge: Why Business Strategy Depends on Productive Friction and Dynamic Specialization* (Boston: Harvard Business School Publishing, 2005). Though the exact term "process orchestration" was not used, these concepts were drawn from a prior paper by Hagel, Durchslag and Brown: John Hagel III, Scott Durchslag, and John Seely Brown, "Orchestrating Loosely Coupled Business Processes: The Secret to Successful Collaboration," October 2002, http://www.johnhagel.com/paper_orchestratingcollaboration.pdf.

10. Victor K. Fung, William K. Fung, and Jerry (Yoram) Wind, *Competing in a Flat World: Building Enterprises for a Borderless World* (Upper Saddle River, NJ: Wharton School Publishing / Pearson Education, 2008), 3.

11. Ibid., 15 (figure 1-4 caption).

12. John Hagel III, Scott Durchslag, and John Seely Brown, "Orchestrating Loosely Coupled Business Processes: The Secret to Successful Collaboration," October 2002, http://www.johnhagel.com/paper_orchestratingcollaboration.pdf.

# Chapter 3

1. Stanley Davis and Christopher Meyer, *Blur: The Speed of Change in the Connected Economy* (Grand Central Publishing, 1999).

2. Carliss Y. Baldwin and Kim B. Clark, *Design Rules: The Power of Modularity*, vol. 1 (Cambridge, MA: MIT Press, 2000). And "Managing in an Age of Modularity," *Harvard Business Review* 75, no. 5 (September–October 1997): 84–93.

3. Stanley Davis and Christopher Meyer, *Blur: The Speed of Change in the Connected Economy* (Grand Central Publishing, 1999).

4. Fung, Fung, and Wind, *Competing in a Flat World*, 3.

5. Thomas Friedman, *The World Is Flat: A Brief History of the Twenty-First Century*, Updated and Expanded Edition (New York: Picador, 2007), 10.

6. Harlan Cleveland and Garry Jacobs, "The Future of Work," *World Academy of Art and Science News*, September 1996, 2, http://www.worldacademy.org/files/September%201996.pdf.

7. Thomas W. Malone, *The Future of Work: How the New Order of Business Will Shape Your Organization, Your Management Style, and Your Life* (Boston: Harvard Business School Press, 2004), 4.

8. Increase in US Industrial R&D Expenditures Reported for 2003 Makes Up for Earlier Decline," National Science Foundation Division of Science Resources Statistics, NSF 06-305, December 2005, http://www.nsf.gov/statistics/infbrief/nsf06305/.

9. U.S. Businesses Report 2008 Worldwide R&D Expense of $330 Billion: Findings from New NSF Survey," National Science Foundation Division of Science Resources Statistics, NSF 10-322, May 2010, http://www.nsf.gov/statistics/infbrief/nsf10322/.

10. Nathan's Battle Foundation, accessed December 7, 2010, http://www.nathansbattle.com/scientific/nclra.html.

11. Roger Longman, "Lilly's Chorus Experiment," IN VIVO 25, no. 2 (February 2007): 35–39.

12. Jeff Davis, NASA, in personal communications and discussion with John Dila and Alpheus Bingham, and Bruce Cragin in personal communication with John Dila, November and December, 2010.

13. Aneesh Chopra, "Rethinking Government" (remarks to the Personal Democracy Forum 2010, Graduate Center, City University of New York, June 4, 2010), http://pdfnyc.civicolive.com/2010/06/04/rethinking-government-with-aneesh-chopra/, and YouTube video, posted June 12, 2010, http://www.youtube.com/watch?v=NbHrLVEUDZE.

# Chapter 4

1. Josh Petersen, January 10, 2005, comment on Chris Anderson, "Definitions: Final Round!," *The Long Tail* (blog), *Wired*, January 9, 2005, http://longtail.typepad.com/the_long_tail/2005/01/definitions_fin.htm.

2. Karim R. Lakhani, Lars Bo Jeppesen, Peter A. Lohse, and Jill A. Panetta, "The Value of Openness in Scientific Problem Solving," Harvard Business School Working Paper, No. 07-050, 2007.

3. Karim R. Lakhani, Lars Bo Jeppesen, Peter A. Lohse, and Jill A. Panetta, "The Value of Openness in Scientific Problem Solving," Harvard Business School Working Paper, no. 07-050 (2007), 3.

4. Julian Birkinshaw and Stuart Crainer, "Combine Harvesting," *Labnotes*, no. 12 (June 2009): 15–18, http://www.managementlab.org/files/site/publications/labnotes/mlab-labnotes-012.pdf.

5. Karim R. Lakhani, Lars Bo Jeppesen, Peter A. Lohse, and Jill A. Panetta, "The Value of Openness in Scientific Problem Solving," Harvard Business School Working Paper, No. 07-050, 2007.

6. James Surowiecki, *The Wisdom of Crowds* (New York: Anchor Books, 2004).

7. Karim Lakhani, in personal communication and discussion with Alpheus Bingham, October 2009.

8. Lars Bo Jeppesen and Karim R. Lakhani, "Marginality and Problem-Solving Effectiveness in Broadcast Search," *Organization Science* 21, no. 5 (September-October 2010): 1016–1033, doi:10.1287/orsc.1090.0491.

9. Neil McLaughlin, "Optimal Marginality: Innovation and Orthodoxy in Fromm's Revision of Psychoanalysis," *Sociological Quarterly* 42, no. 2 (2001): 271-288.

10. Paul R. Carlile, "A Pragmatic View of Knowledge and Boundaries: Boundary Objects in New Product Development," *Organization Science* 13, no. 4 (July-August 2002): 442–455.

11. Chris Anderson, "The Long Tail," *Wired*, no. 12.10 (October 2004), http://www.wired.com/wired/archive/12.10/tail.html.

12. Scott Pegau and John Davis, in personal communications and discussion with Alpheus Bingham, November 2010.

# Chapter 5

1. "Ansari X Prize," X Prize Foundation, http://space.xprize.org/ansari-x-prize.

2. Desk is the company name of a brokering service offering access to global workers mediated through the Internet. The URL for this business' website is www.odesk.com.

3. Gary P. Pisano and Roberto Verganti, "Which Kind of Collaboration Is Right for You?" Harvard Business Review 86, no. 12 (December 2008): 79–86.

4. Eric Bonabeau, "Decisions 2.0: The Power of Collective Intelligence," MIT Sloan Management Review, 50, no. 2 (Winter 2009): 45–52, http://sloanreview.mit.edu/themagazine/articles/2009/winter/50211/decisions-20-the-power-of-collective-intelligence/.

5. Carliss Y. Baldwin and Eric A. Von Hippel, "Modeling a Paradigm Shift: From Producer Innovation to User and Open Collaborative Innovation," Harvard Business School Finance Working Paper 10-038, MIT Sloan Research Paper 4764-09 (August 2010, revised October 5, 2010), http://ssrn.com/abstract=1502864http://ssrn.com/abstract=1502864.

6. John C. Lechleiter (keynote, Brookings Institution Conference on Regional Innovation Clusters: Advancing the Next Economy, Washington, DC, September 23, 2010), http://www.lilly.com/news/speeches/100923/default.html.

7. Roger Longman, "Lilly's Chorus Experiment," IN VIVO 25, no. 2 (February 2007): 35–39.

# Chapter 6

1. Geoffrey C. Bowker, and Susan Leigh Star (1999). *Sorting Things Out: Classification and Its Consequences* (Cambridge, MA: MIT Press, 1999).

2. Christopher A. Bartlett and Sumantra Ghoshal, *Managing Across Borders: The Transnational Solution* (Boston: Harvard Business School Press, 1998).

# Chapter 7

1. IBM, Global CEO Study: The Enterprise of the Future, 2008, http://www.ibm.com/ibm/ideasfromibm/us/ceo/20080505/.

2. As Ronald Coase has pointed out in his work on the nature of the firm and the minimization of transaction costs, which earned him the 1991 Nobel Prize in economics.

3. Drug Discovery World, "e-R&D – the net@work," Alpheus Bingham and Neil Bodick, Spring 2001.

4. Wikipedia, s.v. "culture," accessed October 25, 2010, http://en.wikipedia.org/wiki/Culture.

5. Daniel H. Pink, *Free Agent Nation: The Future of Working for Yourself* (New York: Warner Books, 2001).

6. Economist Intelligence Unit, "Global Firms in 2020: The Next Decade of Change for Organisations and Workers," *Economist*, posted September 16, 2010, http://businessresearch.eiu.com/global-firms-2020.html.

7. Elizabeth Montalbano, "NASA to Crowdsource Software Development," *InformationWeek*, October 14, 2010, http://www.informationweek.com/story/showArticle.jhtml?articleID=227800070.

8. Scott Leibs, "Gaming the System," CFO 24, no. 1 (January 2008), http://www.cfo.com/article.cfm/10345535?f=singlepage.

9. Dave Aron, "Dynamic Collaboration: A Personal Reflection," *Journal of Information Technology* 24, no. 3 (September 2009): 214–218, doi:10.1057/jit.2009.4.

10. "Why We All Want to Grow Towards the Sun," *People Management* 14, no. 11 (May 29, 2008): 42, http://www.peoplemanagement.co.uk/pm/articles/2008/05/why-we-all-want-to-grow-towards-the-sun.htm?EmailSent=true.

11. Graham Warwick, "Can Crowd-Sourcing Spur Aerospace Ideas?," *Aviation Week*, November 8, 2010.

12. Leibs, "Gaming the System."

13. "Wired Magazine's Jeff Howe Talks About Crowdsourcing & TopCoder," TopCoder (blog), posted February 24, 2009.

14. Heather Havenstein, "Eli Lilly Aims to Tap 'Rock Star' Programmers," *Computerworld*, May 14, 2008.

15. "Wired Magazine's Jeff Howe Talks About Crowdsourcing & TopCoder."

16. Julian Birkinshaw and Stuart Crainer, "TopCoder: Open for Competition," Labnotes, no. 8 (May 2008).

17. Mary Brandel, "Should Your Company 'Crowdsource' Its Next Project?" *Computerworld*, December 6, 2007.

18. Leibs, "Gaming the System."

19. Ibid.

# Chapter 8

1. James C. Collins and Jerry I. Porras, "Building Your Company's Vision," *Harvard Business Review*, September-October 1996.

2. Joshua D. Margolis and Mark Wetzel, "Avi Kremer," Harvard Business School Case, 2010, p.5.

3. Ibid.

# Chapter 9

1. President Barack Obama, Transparency and Open Government, January 21, 2009 http://www.whitehouse.gov/the_press_office/Transparency_and_Open_Government/.

2. Ibid.

3. Aneesh Chopra, "Rethinking Government."

4. Rachel Weiner and Arthur Delaney, "Open Government Directive: Obama Moves On Transparency Promise," *Huffington Post*, December 8, 2009, updated March 18, 2010.

5. Ibid.

6. Aliya Sternstein, "One Year In, Resistance to Open Government Memo Lingers," *Nextgov*, January 21, 2010.

7. "Barriers to Changing Government Culture," Opengovwest, last edited March 27, 2010, http://ogw.wikispaces.com/Government+Culture.

8. Peter Orszag, "Promoting Transparency in Government," Office of Management and Budget (blog), Office of Management and Budget, December 8, 2009.

9. Aneesh Chopra, "Empowering All Americans Through Open Government," *Huffington Post*, June 5, 2010.

10. Ibid.

11. Challenge.gov, "Select Prizes and Challenges Launched September 7, 2010 and Featured on Challenge.gov."

12. The White House, *Open Government: A Progress Report to the American People*, 11, December 9, 2009.

13. Ibid, 6.

14. Ibid, 11.

15. Ibid, 4, 5.

# Supplemental Reading

Peter F. Drucker, *Managing in the Next Society* (New York: St. Martin's Press, 2002).

Henry William Chesbrough, *Open Innovation: The New Imperative for Creating and Profiting from Technology* (Boston: Harvard Business Press, 2005).

Stanley Davis and Christopher Meyer, *Blur: The Speed of Change in the Connected Economy* (Grand Central Publishing, 1999).

Don Tapscott and Anthony D. Williams, *Wikinomics: How Mass Collaboration Changes Everything*, Expanded Edition (Portfolio Trade, 2010).

Kevin Kelly, *Out of Control: The New Biology of Machines, Social Systems and the Economic World* (New York: Basic Books, 1995).

John Hagel III and John Seely Brown, *The Only Sustainable Edge: Why Business Strategy Depends on Productive Friction and Dynamic Specialization* (Boston: Harvard Business School Publishing, 2005).

Barry Libert, *Social Nation: How to Harness the Power of Social Media to Attract Customers, Motivate Employees, and Grow Your Business* (Wiley, 2010).

John Hagel III, John Seely Brown, and Lang Davison, *The Power of Pull: How Small Moves, Smartly Made, Can Set Big Things in Motion* (Basic Books, 2010).

Thomas W. Malone, *The Future of Work: How the New Order of Business Will Shape Your Organization, Your Management Style, and Your Life* (Boston: Harvard Business School Press, 2004).

Thomas Friedman, *The World Is Flat: A Brief History of the Twenty-First Century*, Updated and Expanded Edition. (New York: Picador, 2007).

Eric von Hippel, *Democratizing Innovation* (Cambridge: MIT Press, 2005).

James Surowiecki, *The Wisdom of Crowds* (Anchor, 2005).

R. H. Coase, "The Nature of the Firm," *Economica* 4, no. 16 (November 1937): 386–405.

Michael E. Raynor and Jill A. Panetta, "Better Way to R&D," Harvard Business Publishing higher education newsletter, March 15, 2005.

Julian Birkinshaw and Stuart Crainer, "Combine Harvesting," *Labnotes*, no. 12 (June 2009): 15–18.

Karim R. Lakhani, Lars Bo Jeppesen, Peter A. Lohse, and Jill A. Panetta, "The Value of Openness in Scientific Problem Solving," Harvard Business School Working Paper, No. 07-050, 2007.

# INDEX

## A

"a new way to…" archetype, 105-106

accessing talent, potential of open innovation in, 40-42

Action stage (CEO's journey), 207

adapting CDE Playbook, 192-193

ALS (Amyotrophic Lateral Sclerosis) research case study, 193-197

Anderson, Chris, 67, 85

Ansari X PRIZE, 195

Applied Analytical, 96

Apps for Healthy Kids, 217

Arbesman, Harvey, 196

archetypes
"a new way to…," 105-106
"directed stumbling," 104-105
"explore problem solving space," 106-107
"fix MY house," 107-108
"follow the directions," 103-104
"regulated recipe," 103
terminology for, 100-101
"under the radar," 102-103

Archimedes, 82, 84-85

assembly and integration in CDI (Challenge Driven Innovation), 50

Asthmapolis, 217

## B

balancing portfolios, 5, 8

Baldwin, Carliss, 48, 109

Bass, Gary, 216

Bedilion, Tod, 75

behavioral change, preparation for CDE, 188

Bell Labs, 12

Bentham, Jeremy, 31

BHAGs (Big Hairy Audacious Goals), 175

Birkinshaw, Julian, 75, 161

Blockbuster, 212

*Blur: The Speed of Change in the Connected Economy* (Davis and Meyer), 41, 52

Board of Directors, commitment of, 165-169
planning and budgeting, 166-168
securing, 168-169

Bonabeau, Eric, 109

boundary objects, 84, 123

Bradin, David, 82

broadcast search
characteristics of the crowd, 77-81
*serendipity and challenge presentation, 82-86*
*tear gas example, 81-82*

# W–Z

**FINANCIAL TIMES**

In an increasingly competitive world, it is quality of thinking that gives an edge—an idea that opens new doors, a technique that solves a problem, or an insight that simply helps make sense of it all.

We work with leading authors in the various arenas of business and finance to bring cutting-edge thinking and best-learning practices to a global market.

It is our goal to create world-class print publications and electronic products that give readers knowledge and understanding that can then be applied, whether studying or at work.

To find out more about our business products, you can visit us at www.ftpress.com.